best Wisconsin bike trips

Designed by William T. Pope
Map design by Frenchtown Studios
Editing by Editorial Solutions
Editorial and production manager, Susan Pigorsch
Typeset by Fleetwood Graphics, Madison, WI
Printed by American Printing, Madison, WI

Published 1985

Wisconsin Trails, Inc.
P.O. Box 5650
Madison, Wisconsin 53705

First printing 1985
Second printing 1986
Third printing 1988

Printed in the United States of America

ISBN 0-915024-29-2

Library of Congress Cataloging in Publication Data

Van Valkenberg, Phil, 1945-
   Best Wisconsin bike trips.

1. Bicycle touring--Wisconsin--Guide-books.
2. Wisconsin--Description and travel--1981-Guide books.   I. Title.
GV1045.5.W6V35 1985   917.75'0443   85-5329
ISBN 0-915024-29-2 (pbk.)

BEFORE YOU RIDE

PLANNING YOUR BIKE TRIP

Do you want to bike a few miles, stop at a state park, and tour through a historic home? Or would you rather spend a whole day off-road on one of the state bike trails? No matter what you're looking for, this guide will help you design bike trips that match your interests and abilities.

Read the text and examine the map symbols to find points of interest that appeal to you. For example, you might choose a start or finish point at the end of a loop near a restaurant. The solid dots along the routes are mile markers. Count them to figure how long a loop is or how far it is to the next intersection. To help you find or avoid hilly country, contour lines and elevations are noted where appropriate. If a road runs parallel to contour lines or a river or stream, it is probably a level area. If it crosses the contour lines you will either be going up or downhill.

Distance and difficulty of terrain should be weighed against the day's riding conditions as well as the bicyclist's abilities. Wind and heat are significant factors. A strong wind will never help you as much as it will hinder you; however, you can plan your travel to out-fox the wind. On nice summer days in Wisconsin, the wind is usually out of the southwest, and blows strongly from late morning until an hour or so before sunset. On such a day ride west in the early morning when the wind is calm; then let the wind help blow you east in the afternoon.

The effect of the air temperature is compounded by the wind. A hot wind can dehydrate and a cool wind can chill. In the heat, be sure to keep your head covered and drink frequently from your water bottle. In cool weather, dress warmly. It's important to keep your head, chest, and knees warm. Remember, if your route takes you near a large body of water like the Great Lakes, you may find much cooler temperatures.

In choosing a route, also consider traffic volume and types of road surface. Gravel roads will, for the most part, be of interest only to fat-tired and mountain-bike riders. Fortunately gravel and paved town roads have little motor vehicle traffic and offer relaxed riding for bicyclists of all ages and abilities. On county, state and federal highways, the greater traffic volumes should be taken into account. Numbers in boxes indicate the most recent 24-hour traffic count on the adjacent roadway. I consider roads with less than 500 vehicles per day to be ideal for almost everyone. The exceptions are young children who should learn riding skills on off-road bike trails and be kept away from roads with more than 300 vehicles per day.

Busy roads with paved shoulders are an obvious safety improvement, but only to a certain extent. These roads tend to have lots of trucks, which, at highway speeds, have a dangerous wind-blast effect on bicycles. To impress you with the inadvisability of considering major highways as possible shortcuts, I've included their traffic counts as well. Where it is necessary to use a stretch of one of these heavily traveled roads, I recommend riding or walking your bike on the shoulder.

Because you may not be able to find food and water in an unincorporated town, it is a good idea to carry some energy snacks with you as well as water.

Make advance reservations for lodging and camping wherever possible. Campsite reservations may be necessary if you plan to arrive by car. Campers arriving by bicycle are now accomodated at all state parks in special areas without advance reservations. For further information contact: Wisconsin Department of Natural Resources, P.O. Box 7921, Madison, WI 53707

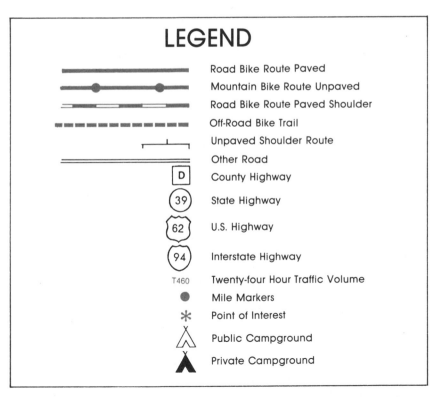

LEGEND

———	Road Bike Route Paved
●——●——	Mountain Bike Route Unpaved
—▭——▭—	Road Bike Route Paved Shoulder
■ ■ ■ ■	Off-Road Bike Trail
⌐___⌐	Unpaved Shoulder Route
═══════	Other Road
D	County Highway
39	State Highway
62	U.S. Highway
94	Interstate Highway
T460	Twenty-four Hour Traffic Volume
●	Mile Markers
✳	Point of Interest
⛺	Public Campground
▲	Private Campground

AN EXTENDED BIKE TRIP NETWORK

Have you ever dreamed about taking a bicycle vacation? The feeling of freedom and adventure of such a trip is hard to match. At the same time such an expedition is relatively easy to undertake. If you have a song in your heart and time on your hands consider hitting the road on the Extended Bike Trip Network. The New Glarus-Sugar River Trail, Military Ridge Trail, Mineral Point, Spring Green, Spring Valley, Natural Bridge and Devil's Lake rides are all linked together by lightly trafficked connecting roads. You'll be able to explore six state parks, two state bike trails, numerous campgrounds and historical sites plus lots of great scenery. On each of these seven bike trip maps you will find directions showing the roads and indicating the miles to an adjacent route. You can custom tailor a tour just right for the condition of your legs and your spirit of adventure.

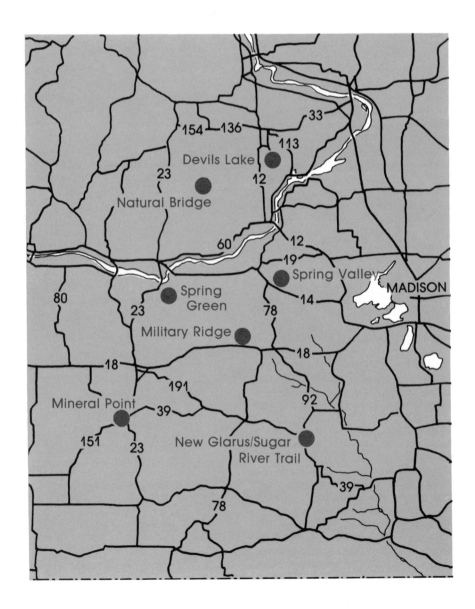

ACHES AND PAINS

The smooth rotary movement of bicycling makes it one of the least punishing forms of exercise. If you are a casual rider you may never have any problems. People who push themselves to faster speeds or try for long distances may encounter difficulties from improper technique, riding position, warm-up, clothing and equipment. Take heart. There are remedies.

Bike shorts or seamless apparel of some sort should be used. Cleanliness of body and clothing is essential. Once an infection begins, your riding ends.

Knee trouble can stem from a number of things. Most ten-speeds come equipped with a 100 inch top gear and there are probably not more than several hundred cyclists in the country who have the ability to pedal a gear that high for any length of time. Riders who push gears that are too high are pushing their knees beyond their limits. Smooth out your pedaling. If you want to go faster, spin the pedals faster rather than shifting into a higher gear. That way you divide up the work and won't overload your knees. Efficiency is the name of the game. You don't have to feel like you are working hard to do hard work on a bicycle.

Improper riding position can also cause knee trouble. You may be too far forward over the pedals or may be straightening out your knees too much or not enough (Fig. 1 & 2). Improper warm-up or inadequate clothing can spell knee disaster. The circulation in your joints takes a while to get going, so *always* pedal in low gears for the first two miles, further in cool weather. Anytime the temperature is below 65 degrees, leg clothing must be worn. I recommend seamless tights, long underwear or dancers' leg warmers (which can be slipped off easily if the temperature rises). For those marginal days or for cool mornings and prolonged head winds, rub Ben-Gay on your knees, then cover with a layer of Vaseline. Vaseline alone is good too. Don't underestimate the importance of this easy, convenient method of knee protection.

Foot pain commonly results from hard riding in soft-soled shoes. Bicycle shoes offer a stiff, comfortable platform for your feet. Used with cleats, they make walking difficult, but there are versatile special stiff-soled shoes available.

Numbness or pain in the palm of the hand can plague long-distance riders. Two factors contribute here: stiff-arming and single-hand position. Keep your elbows bent; that way they work like shock absorbers. If you ride with stiff arms your bones act like jackhammers on the nerves in your palms. If you lack the strength to ride with elbows flexed, do some simple weight exercises to strengthen your triceps.

Changing your hand position frequently is also important. Ten-speed-type handlebars and brake levers are designed to offer a variety of positions (Fig. 3-7). Bicycle gloves are helpful and many people use padded handlebar grips, but the only real cure is proper use of the handlebars.

Getting to the seat of the matter, I am sorry to say there are no pat answers for you saddle-sore riders. Remember that everyone is different, so a saddle that is perfect for one may be uncomfortable for another. You will have to experiment to find the right one for you. The sit test on showroom or friends' bikes is a good way to start. What feels good is worth a try.

Cost and construction of saddle models on the market are not good barometers of comfort. Of the 15 leather

Fig. 1—Your knees should not be too forward in relation to the pedal. With the cranks horizontal, a plumb line held at the top of your shin bone should always pass behind the pedal axle.

Fig. 2—Saddle height shold be low enough to allow a slight bend to your leg at the bottom of the crank rotation when you place your heel on the pedal. Saddles too high, too low, or too far forward cause knee pains on long rides.

Fig. 3 Seated downhill position

Fig. 4 Seated uphill position

Fig. 5 Standing uphill position

Fig. 6 Sprinting position

Fig. 7 Seated touring position

and synthetic saddles I have tried, the material used was consistently insignificant in regard to comfort. The amount of riding you do also makes a difference.

Riding position must be correct for successful results. The saddle should be level, though it can be varied a few degrees either way. Give any new saddle a chance, as this partnership between two alien forms takes time.

FICKLE FLATS

Flats are diabolical. They happen to the best equipment and at the worst times. You may go thousands of miles without one and then have five in a week. The chances that your bike trip will come to a sudden halt are also multiplied by the number of people participating.

The only way to cheat the puncture demon is to be prepared. Before you leave, check tires for cuts, bulges, embedded bits of metal or glass, and proper pressure. Bulges and serious cuts require immediate replacement of the tire. Remove imbedded objects. If the tube continues to hold air go ahead and ride on it.

If you use sew-up tires just bring along one or two easy-to-carry spares. For the more conventional wire-on tires, folding spare tires with fiberglass beads are offered by several manufacturers. Although it is a good idea to also have a spare tube available for extended trips, being prepared to patch the tube is the most reasonable step to follow. I don't care for the aerosol liquid-repair inflation systems. If they fail they leave an incredible mess and preclude futher repair efforts.

Assemble the tools and supplies you need along with a good, portable pump. The following procedure for fixing a flat can be employed at home or on the road.

Tools: Tire pump (Fig. 1 & 2)
Axlenut wrenches (if hubs are bolt-on type)
Tire irons
Patch kit
Valve tool
File

Parts: Tube
Tire (replacement must be exactly the same)
Rim Strip

Time: 10-25 minutes

Preparation: Is your tire really flat? Tubes lose air gradually at the rate of 2 to 6 pounds a week. if you've not used your

A flat tire can be irritating even to the seasoned bicycle tourist.

Fig.1—A good pump and a few tools will give you the confidence to ride anywhere.

bike for some time, this may be the cause of the flat. Reinflate.

Check for a loose valve. (With schroeder valves—the type generally used for bicycles, autos, and motorcycles— a loose valve is a common cause of flats.) Inflate tire. lick your finger and spread the saliva over the valve. If a bubble begins to form in about ten seconds, you have a loose valve. Tighten it with valve tightening tool and recheck. If the leak continues, replace the valve.

Valve tools and valves are available at service stations. A very handy valve tool is the type that doubles as a valve cap. Incidentally, a valve cap does not seal the valve, but does keep it clean and working properly.

Step 1: Remove the wheel.

Remove quick-release wheels by opening the lever until it is perpendicular to the wheel. In the case of a rear wheel, the chain should be on the smallest sprocket to facilitate removal. As you push the rear wheel forward, swing the rear derailleur back and the wheel should drop out. (Many bikes have quick-release levers on the brakes that open up the brake pads slightly to allow an inflated tire to pass between the rubbers. Disengage this lever.)

Remove bolt-on wheels by turning the axle nuts counterclockwise. Use a wrench on each side and loosen both simultaneously. If you have only one wrench, turn each nut until it moves just slightly, then loosen both nuts alternately so you don't affect the bearing adjustment.

Step 2: Check the outside of the tire. Look for and remove any tack, staple, nail or piece of glass.

Step 3: Remove the tire (Fig. 3)

Use tire irons or smooth silverware handles. (Screwdrivers or other sharp-edged objects may cut the cords of the tire, causing a blowout in the future.) Make sure that the tube is completely deflated. Squeeze the tire together all the way around the wheel, freeing it from the rim.

Insert a tire iron between the tire and rim *near the valve* and begin prying one side of the tire over the rim edge. Hold the first iron in position with one hand and insert the second iron about 5 inches

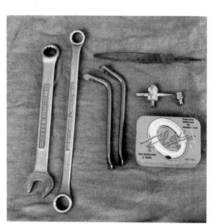

Fig. 2—Wrenches for bolt-on hubs, tire irons, small file, valve tool and cap, and patch kit.

from the first. Continue holding the first iron and move another 5 inches with the second iron. After a few times you should be able to peel one side of the tire over the rim edge all the way around.

Pull the tube, except for the valve, out of the tire casing. Lift or pry the other side of the tire from the rim. Push the valve stem out of the rim and remove the tube.

Step 4: Find the hole (Fig. 4)

This step is important even if you are going to replace the tube, unless a puncture-causing object was found during Step 2.

Inflate the tube to about twice its normal size. Form a circle around the tube with your thumb and forefinger. By moving the tube slowly through this circle, you should be able to feel the air escaping at the point of puncture. If you think you have found the spot but are not sure, hold that part of the tube close to your lips, where your skin is more sensitive.

Mark the spot.

Step 5: Find the cause.

If no external cause was found in Step 2, note whether the hole in the tube is on the part that rests against the rim or the tire casing.

If the puncture is on the rim side, inspect the rim. The most common cause is a rim strip (large rubber or cloth band)

that is not adequately covering the spoke ends. If so reposition or replace the rim strip. (I recommend replacing cloth rim strips with rubber ones.) Look for rough or rusted spots in the rim and clean them with a file, taking care to eliminate all shavings.

If the tube puncture is on the side that rests against the tire casing, inspect the inside of the tire. Move your fingers around the inside of the casing. *Go slow:* You are looking for a sharp protrusion.

Visually inspect the inside of the tire casing. You will be able to see the threadlike cords that give the tire its strength. If more than 2 cords have been

Fig. 3—Make your first pry near the valve.

Fig. 4—Pass the reinflated tube through your thumb and forefinger to feel for escaping air.

cut, you should consider replacing the tire.

Step 6: Patch the tube.

If the hole is within a half inch of the valve, patching will not work. Your patch kit should contain: patches and patch material, glue and a piece of sandpaper or filelike metal. (Sometimes the file is stamped into the kit cover.)

Cut a patch large enough to overlap the puncture three-eighths of an inch all around. Roughen an area around the puncture *a little larger* than the selected patch. Scuff the area in two directions and afterwards do not touch the spot with your fingers. Apply a *very thin* layer of glue to the scuffed area and let dry for minute or two. If it takes longer, you used too much glue.

Peel back the protective sheeting on the patch, apply the patch without touching its sticky surface, and pound it or roll over it with a smooth object to ensure a seal. Touch the excess glue area or dust it with talcum powder to prevent it from sticking to the tire casing.

Step 7: Replace the tube (Fig. 5)

Inflate the tube just enough to give it shape and stuff it inside the tire casing. Insert the valve into the wheel rim. Work the first side of the tire over the rim edge by hand. Never use tire irons when re-

Fig. 5—When you replace the tube and tire, use only your hands and end up at the valve.

Bicycling safely on the open road requires common sense and a conscientious effort.

mounting a tire. You don't need them and you run a large risk of creating a new puncture or an abrasion that will later become a leak.

To get the second side of the tire on, start *opposite* the valve. Work with both hands around the tire, moving toward the valve. Getting the tire over the rim edge near the valve may be difficult. Use one hand to hold your ground and squeeze together all the way around the part of the tire that is already on. This allows the edge of the tire to drop into the channel in the center of the rim. You should be able to roll the remainder of the tire over the rim edge.

Make sure the valve is straight. If not, shift the tire around.

Step 8: Inflate the tire.

Push the valve partway down into the valve hole. This frees the tube if it has become caught between the tire and rim edge. Inflate the tube to about 20 pounds. If the tire is not on the rim evenly, deflate the tube and shift the tire around.

Inflate the tube to proper pressure and check to see if the tire has moved into proper position. If not, overinflate by 10 to 20 pounds to pop it out. If this fails, deflate and put a little soapy water (never use oil) on the area and try again.

Step 9: Replace the wheel.

Slip the tire between the brake rubbers (be careful not to knock them out of their holders), and slide the axle into the fork ends. For a front wheel, center the wheel in the fork by moving the axle to the bottom of the fork slot.

For a rear wheel, move the axle all the way back on the derailleur side, then place your index fingers between the rim and chain-stay frame tubes on each side. When you think the wheel is centered, wrap your right thumb around one spoke and hold the wheel in position against your forefinger while you use your left hand to close the quick-release or slightly snug the axle nut.

If you have quick-release you are finished. If bolt-on, switch hands and slightly snug the right nut. Using two wrenches, tighten the nuts evenly. With one wrench, alternately snug the nuts until both are secure.

Step 10: Check over.

Check your rear derailleur adjustment. Re-engage the brake quick-release if you have one. Be certain that the brake rubbers are contacting the rim properly and are not rubbing.

SAFETY IS SELF-PRESERVATION

Bicyclists have always had the same rights to enjoy the public roadways as the operators of other types of vehicles. But the growing popularity of bicycling has spurred improvements in both equipment and riding environments enhancing the safety of the sport. Due to the increase in the numbers of bicyclists, motorists are better able to cope with the presence of two-tired vehicles, and a state-wide policy of paving shoulders of heavily-traveled roads and expanding off-road bicycle paths has enhanced safety. Bicycle quality has been upgraded along with the availability of professional maintenance.

Today we have better and, in some cases, completely new, safety equipment. Lighting and reflector systems, high-visibility and reflective bicycling clothing, effective eyeglass-mounted rearview mirrors, and newly-developed protective head gear have all been important advances. However, in spite of these improvements, each bicycling season produces a new crop of serious injuries and deaths. In the final analysis, hardly any of these were truly accidents. All the improvements in bicycling environment and protective equipment mean little if you don't have the attitude that safety should be your foremost consideration. Safety is still and always will be self-preservation. Mutual respect and consideration for everyone on our roadways is essential.

• **Wear bright clothing**—Visibility is your first line of defense, day or night. Clothes that are brightly colored or patterned present a contrast to your surroundings and give motorists advance warning of your presence on the roadway. Wear reflectorized clothing at night and make sure your bike has a good light and adequate reflectors.

• **Obey traffic laws**—Since the bicycle is considered a vehicle, most of the laws affecting bicycles are the same as for motor vehicles. Your responsibility to be familiar with and to obey all such regulations is every bit as great and important as that of motor vehicle operators.

• **Stay aware of the traffic environment**—Listen for the approach of overtaking vehicles and ride in a straight and steady manner. Remember that there may be more than one vehicle associated with the sound. Assume that drivers approaching an intersection have not seen you. Wait for direct eye contact to be absolutely sure they will yield.

• **Ride as far to the right as possible**— You must ride on the right side of the roadway and you should stay as close to the edge of the pavement as its condition will allow. Your speed and riding skill will be a factor in determining this position. If paved shoulders are present, use them and stay out of the traffic stream.

• **Avoid riding at night and in inclement weather**—Bicycling on rural roads at night is the single most hazardous situation. Drinking and driving motorists are a widespread problem compounding the danger. Lights and high-visibility reflective equipment and clothing are imperative at night and in bad weather.

• **Keep your equipment in good working order**—Equipment failure is a common contributing factor in bicycle accidents. If you do not know how to maintain your bike properly consult a professional at a bicycle shop. If you do have these skills, take responsibility for the other members of your group.

• **Make all stops off the roadway**—If you stop to rest or wait, move your bike completely off the pavement. If a motorist has to make an instant decision between hitting an oncoming truck or a bicycle, you can bet it won't be the truck.

• **Communicate with traffic and companions**—Use hand signals to show motorists and fellow bicyclists you intend to turn. Warn your companions vocally of the approach of other vehicles. Do not let the overall safety of your group conform to the lowest common denominator. If you find your companion's safety practices inadequate, say something about it.

• **Polish your bicycling skills**—Operating a bicycle is something usually learned in childhood and often not given much more thought than learning to walk. This attitude can lead to disaster. Bicycling safely in the environment of the open road requires skills that come from practice and conscientious effort.

THE CANINE FACTOR

Dogs are not the only animals you will encounter in the roadway, but they are probably the most common. And, when you find yourself facing a dog in the road, you're in a serious situation.

An intentional dog attack is very rare. In fifteen years of rural riding I have only been bitten twice. Most dogs respond to simple authoritarian commands such as "stay" or "go home" and these are your first lines of defense. Dogs respond better to these commands if they are issued before their pursuit has really begun, so keep a sharp eye for dogs up ahead. If the animal responds to your commands, be sure to follow them up with "good dog." If you are riding fast enough to escape a chasing dog all is well and good unless you have friends coming up behind.

If speaking to the dog or running away does not work, there are several alternatives. Throughout the incident make sure you continue to concentrate on the task of bicycling so you are not surprised by traffic: stay on your side of the road or on the road period. Slow to a stop and get off the bike, keeping it between you and the dog. This eliminates the fun of the pursuit. Continue to issue commands. You may want to equip yourself with a commercially available dog repellent or a squeeze bottle containing a solution of one part ammonia and two parts water, or menace the dog with your bike or pump. For your safety, these methods should be attempted only when stopped. Stand your ground, but never chase a dog either off the roadway or onto private property. Dogs are territorial animals and could suddenly attack you to defend their homestead. Make sure every one in your group is familiar with these methods of action. After things have calmed down, walk your bike away from the dog for a distance before remounting.

If you or a friend is bitten, find the owner if possible and see if the animal has had rabies shots. Report the incident along with the owner's name, the location and a description of the dog to the local sheriff's office. If the dog has not had shots, the sheriff must impound it for a period of two weeks for observation. Get a tetanus shot as soon as possible. A letter to the local chamber of commerce about any incident, even one about a particulary belligerent dog that did not bite, is also a good idea.

THE MOUNTAIN BIKE

A WHOLE NEW BIKING GAME

The trend towards lighter, faster road bicycles did much to revive the popularity of biking, both for transportation and recreation. But at the same time, these sleek ten-speeds limited riders to the linear confines of blacktopped roads.

It wasn't until the early '70's in California that kids rediscovered the fun of fat-tired bicycles and traffic-free environments. They began modifying the then-popular Sting Ray bikes for off-road use. These evolved into BMX (bicycle motorcross) bicycles, and later, into the innovative mountain bike.

The biggest fans of these new machines are road bicyclists, who are finding new challenge and adventure on traffic-free roads and trails. Mountain bikes are also exciting older people, who never liked the skinny tires and funny, forward-leaning handlebars of ten-speeds in the first place, and urban cyclists, who find that fat-tired bikes can handle the potholes and rough roads that used to send them to the repair shop. Farmers, hunters, and fishermen are discovering mountain bikes too—they are silent, reasonably priced, and easily transported over fences or fallen trees.

Some people may still wonder why these bikes that came out of the American West would catch on in a bicycle-friendly state like Wisconsin, with its 60,000 miles of lightly-traveled, paved back roads. The reason is this: there are also 35,000 miles of gravel roads in the state—used only by a few cars a day—plus hundreds of miles of forest and cross-country trails suitable for mountain biking.

Marvelous sights, which you would never see from a road bicycle, await you in *Best Wisconsin Bike Trips*. Fascinating, out-of-the-way places are notated both on the maps and in the narratives to guide fat-tired riders.

Fig. 1—Padding on the top tube is a help if you must carry your bike over fallen trees.

Fig. 2-3—Rock your bike from side to side for effective, out-of-the-saddle climbing.

GETTING THE MOST OUT OF YOUR MOUNTAIN BIKE

Fig. 4—Position your hands close to the stem for in-the-saddle uphill grinds.

Fig. 5—On rough surfaces, put your weight on your feet, and shift your weight back on the downhills.

Mountain bikes are only a refinement of existing, time-tested bicycle designs. If used in the same way and in the same places that you use a normal bike, you need not expand your riding expertise—you must merely get acquainted with the different brake and shift lever positions on the handle bars.

The real appeal of mountain bikes lies beyond the pale of civilized biking. These machines are meant to go offroad, which involves more than just pushing pedals around. Mountain biking is challenging, rather like cross-country skiing, and a little movement here or there makes a big difference.

The type of surface you are on will often determine the necessary technique. On a rocky uphill you will want to keep your pedal rpms up so you have some reserve power if you lose speed. On a level surface, on the other hand, you will be more comfortable in a high-gear, placing lots of pressure on the pedals and resting on the saddle and handle bars. Staying relaxed and confident in the inherent stability of your bike is all-important.

Braking on a rough surface is always best done intermittently, if possible. Your forks and spokes are the bike's suspension system, and applying the brakes in effect unites the wheel rims to the frame forming a rigid unit, which short circuits the bike's shock-absorbing character. When bumping your front wheel over any sizable object, make sure you have completed the braking process before the encounter—otherwise you will be meeting it with a solid object rather than a free rolling wheel. Be sure you have finished braking before entering a corner also, or if you must brake use the rear one only. Your best traction will be had by moving forward onto the tip of the saddle and pedalling through the corner. On a long or extremely steep downhill run you can lower your center of gravity by using the quick release seat post binder to drop the saddle height down.

Conditioning is a critical factor in climbing steep hills, and there is really no substitute. But the right technique will help you make the most of what energy you have. Again, the surface you're riding and its steepness makes a difference. Given adequate traction you may want to climb out of the saddle. Rocking the bike is essential to efficient pumping. This is done by pulling up on the left hand grip as you push down on the left pedal and vice versa (see figures 2 & 3). This brings your arm and upper body strength into play to help push the pedals down. As you can see from the photos, it also places your center of gravity more directly over the pedal. From a traction stand point, a slightly lower gear is best.

If an obstacle presents itself, hustle the bike with a few quick rocks back and forth to get your speed up a little. This way you will have the same speed after you clear the obstacle as you did before you speeded up—you won't find yourself coming out of it in a desperate anerobic crunch.

You can improve out-of-saddle traction by shifting your weight back, but this is only useful for short hills. I prefer carrying any gear on a rear rack of panniers for reasons of increased traction.

On extremely steep, loose-surfaced or long hills you will have to climb in the saddle for reasons of traction or to relieve the strain of pumping (Fig.4). If the pitch is radical you will have to lean forward to keep the front wheel from coming off the ground. I glued some handlebar padding material on close to the stem so I could use the position shown in Figure 4 as I would on a road bike. This brings the back muscles into play and is very effective in an all-out, uphill effort. The padding also offers an alternate hand position to help stave off hand and wrist fatigue on a long ride. Padding on the underside of the top tube near the saddle is also a good idea if you'll be biking in rough areas, where bikes must be carried over fallen trees, etc. (Fig.1).

MOUNTAIN BIKE SAFETY

Caution and foresight are as important as leg strength in off-road riding. Ruts parallel to your path of travel are hazards that can throw you to the ground in an instant. If your wheel drops into a deep rut, brake to a stop immediately. If you try to ride through or climb out, the front wheel will jam up and you will leave the bike via an over-the-handlebar route.

If you have to ride over broom-handle thick sticks or branches, make sure you cross them close to their mid-sections. Hitting one near its end can flip it up into your spokes, resulting in the above mentioned phenomenon. I recommend wearing a good helmet for off-road work.

Getting back from a trip in one piece is an important consideration for off-road bicyclists. The next important consideration is getting back period. The forest is a confusing place at best and even if you know where the sun should be, trees or unexpected clouds may obscure it. Sometimes well-marked cross-country trail systems can be difficult to follow in summer, when a myriad of trails and logging roads, which would not even be noticed under winter snows, suddenly present themselves. Never start biking on unfamiliar trails late in the day and always carry a compass. I like the pin-on hunter's compass that can be easily referred to before you are lost. If you don't know how to use a compass, learn before you have to rely on it.

Mechanical or electronic odometers are also recommended as the riding surface and terrain can vary your speed considerably and distort your sense of distance. Electronic odometers are nice because most have a kilometer mode, and cross-country trail systems are commonly marked in kilometers, roughly two-thirds of a mile. Six kilometers is about four miles. I find myself averaging four to six miles per hour on extremely rough trails, six to ten on moderate off-road terrain and ten to 14 on gravel or paved roads. This compares with the 15 to 19 miles per hour I usually travel on my road bike.

You're not likely to find the hungry and thirsty bicyclist's savior, the cross-roads tavern, on any off-road trails, so be sure you start out with a full water bottle and some energy food. A fanny pack is a good way to carry snacks, maps and small items of clothing. What you wear can also make the difference between an enjoyable ride and a trial. Your shoes should have a firm sole, and padded gloves will minimize fatigue. The mountain bike saddle is actually less irritating than a road bike's seat because you will be standing on the pedals and just generally pushing much more, thereby taking pressure off the seat. Keep in mind that the chamois on regular bike shorts is in the wrong place for an upright riding position; you will be happier with what are usually called touring shorts. Don't forget insect repellent during the summer months. It is not always possible to ride faster than the critters.

A map, compass and odometer are essential for off-road riding.

OFF-ROAD ETHICS

When the bicyclist leaves the roadway for the trail, a metamorphosis takes place. On the road the bicycle is the most vulnerable vehicle in the traffic mix and depends on the respect of motor vehicle users. Off-road, the bicyclist becomes the most potentially dangerous presence. If the responsibility that necessarily must be attached to this status is ignored, we will soon see "No Bicycling" signs posted in front of our favorite trails.

In the process of nosing out places to ride mountain bikes, I rejected many areas because of a single fault: potential conflict with existing types of recreation. As you can tell from looking over the places I have recommended, there is a wealth of trails where mountain bikers can enjoy a real off-road experience without infringing on the enjoyment of others. Many recommended cross-country trail systems are also hiking trails during the summer, and although they are wide enough to accomodate a bicyclist and a pedestrian, keep in mind that you could generate animosity by zipping by even if there were no apparent danger. Moderate your speed and communicate so that hikers are aware of your presence.

"Posted: No Hunting or Trespassing" signs do apply to mountain bikers. If you ignore them you are violating the law as well as making a bad name for all bicyclists. If a certain posted lane seems irresistable, take the time to find the owner and ask permission. You may make a friend and find out about other places to ride as well.

The human-powered wheel is certainly much easier on a trail surface than its motorized counterpart or horses hooves, and I would venture that in most situations where adequate width exists, bikes have less impact than a hiking boot. Unless a hillside or trail is nursing a struggling plant community, the steepness or softness of the surface will usually impede pedaling before any damage is done. Still, it is possible to harm trail surfaces if you are not sensitive to particular existing conditions. Sensitivity is the key. We must take care to ensure that these bikes, which have opened up a new world of riding, do not detract from the environment or its enjoyment by others.

CHOOSING *A MOUNTAIN* BIKE

After two thousand miles of mountain biking, I've checked out lots of different brands, and I feel knowledgeable enough to give advice. The first thing to consider is the type of use you expect to give your bike. If your interest is in a more durable, commuting bike to use on gravel road shoulders or unpaved bike paths, most any of the available models will do. There's a considerable increase in durability from the fat tires alone. Longer excursions on gravel roads over hilly terrain will make lightweight components and more efficient, longer-wearing bearings something to consider.

When we start talking about real off-road riding, quality becomes important for reasons of safety. Rough riding puts stresses on bicycles that road riding never will. The frame and fork tubes should be of top quality, heavy-gage chrome molybdenum. When riding on an old logging trail, such as those in the national forests, drive train components can take a beating: swagged cranks come loose, lightweight chains break and road derailleurs self-destruct. Specially designed and constructed mountain bike derailleurs have unique methods of action that allow them to shift well under the most highly stressed situations. Pedals should be of sturdy construction and have a surface that grips well into the shoe sole. I don't recommend toe clips for most off-road riding.

The integrity of the parts that stop you are as important as the parts that make you go. All good mountain bike brakes I have seen are of cantilever design, meaning that the brake arm pivots are joined directly to the fork tubes or seat stays. High-quality seat posts and handlebar stems are essential, and a quick release feature for vertical adjustment of the saddle is desirable. If you expect to ride a lot, sealed bearings in the hubs and bottom bracket are worth the investment.

Proper fit of your mountain bike is crucial. Because these bikes have greater ground clearance, you'll probably take a frame that is about two inches smaller than your road bike. You absolutely must have an inch or more of clearance between your crotch and the top tube. A foam pad on the top tube is also recommended. Other important accessories are a sturdy, well-mounted water bottle cage and a rear carrier rack. A map holder and mechanical or electronic odometer are always useful and sometimes essential. Fenders are very welcome accessories if you want to ride anytime and anywhere.

30 BEST
WISCONSIN
BIKE TRIPS

MILITARY RIDGE RIDE

In *Vandermark's Folly*, author Herbert Quick gives a fascinating description of the route: "The road was rutted, poached deep where wet and beaten hard where dry, or pulverized into dust by the stream of emigration. Here we went . . . blue jeans, corduroys, rags, tatters, silks, satins, caps, tall hats, poverty, riches; speculators, missionaries, land-hunters, merchants; . . . so far from civilization, shot out of civilization by the forces of civilization itself."

Time has changed the ridge. Before farmers broke the prairie sod with the newly developed steel plow, there were hundreds of animal-shaped Indian mounds on the route between the Mississippi River and Lake Mendota. These were the work of a culture that disappeared some 700 years ago. Remnants of the prairie ecology, notably the tall bluestem grasses, exist now only along the old railroad right-of-way. But the cone-shaped silhouette of Blue Mounds, rising 500 feet above the level of the ridge, still beckons today's traveler as it always has. It is from a distance that its wooded slopes appear to be blue. Today the trail connects quaint towns and state parks rather than military forts. You can camp, hike, swim and relax at special campgrounds for bicyclists at Governor Dodge or Blue Mounds state parks.

The towns: Verona, Riley, Mount Horeb, Blue Mounds, Barneveld, Ridgeway and Dodgeville, all strung out at intervals of less than six miles, offer a Wisconsin sampler of taverns, drive-ins, cafes and bakeries. Riley is not a town in the normal sense. It is a town in the Wisconsin sense, meaning it is a small cluster of buildings around a tavern. The Riley Tavern is by no means an ordinary establishment. It has been a popular destination for bicyclists for years, and the destination of the annual New Years Day bike ride from Madison. Instead of a TV, you'll find a juke box featuring such old-time favorites as "Charlie's Shoes" and "Footprints in the Snow." Your quarter will buy you five plays. More than

just a watering hole, the Riley Tavern is a relic from a different time. On the first Saturday of the month the lawn in front of the tavern is the scene of an informal bluegrass music jamboree.

Thanks to the Wisconsin Department of Natural Resources, you can now pedal on a traffic-free trail on one of the oldest avenues of travel in the state—Military Ridge. It is the only relatively level east-west route south of the Wisconsin River between Madison and the Mississippi. The abandonment of the Chicago and Northwestern Railroad and the acquisition of the grade from Dodgeville to Madison made this top-of-the-world ride possible. The adjacent highway has far too much traffic and the alternative town and county roads offer an endless succession of 400-foot climbs.

Glacial winds left their mark on the

ridge, laying down a fine layer of loess, the dust from the grinding of the ice sheets. It made a fertile soil for the waving prairie grasses that soon stretched from horizon to horizon. Indians, who first used the ridge as a trail, maintained this game-rich environment by periodically burning it. Fire-resistant burr oaks still stand as prairie hallmarks.

In 1835, the U.S. Army, under the command of future president, Zachary Taylor, widened the trail for a section of a road (Prairie du Chien to Poynette) that would eventually connect the frontier forts at Prairie du Chien, Portage and Green Bay. Its completion encouraged the influx of settlers pursuing the promise of the West.

If you arrive too late to try a macaroon at Gobles Bakery and Cafe in Mount Horeb, you will have to visit again; I have

Listen to bluegrass at the Riley Tavern on the first Saturday of the month — or stop anytime for food and drink.

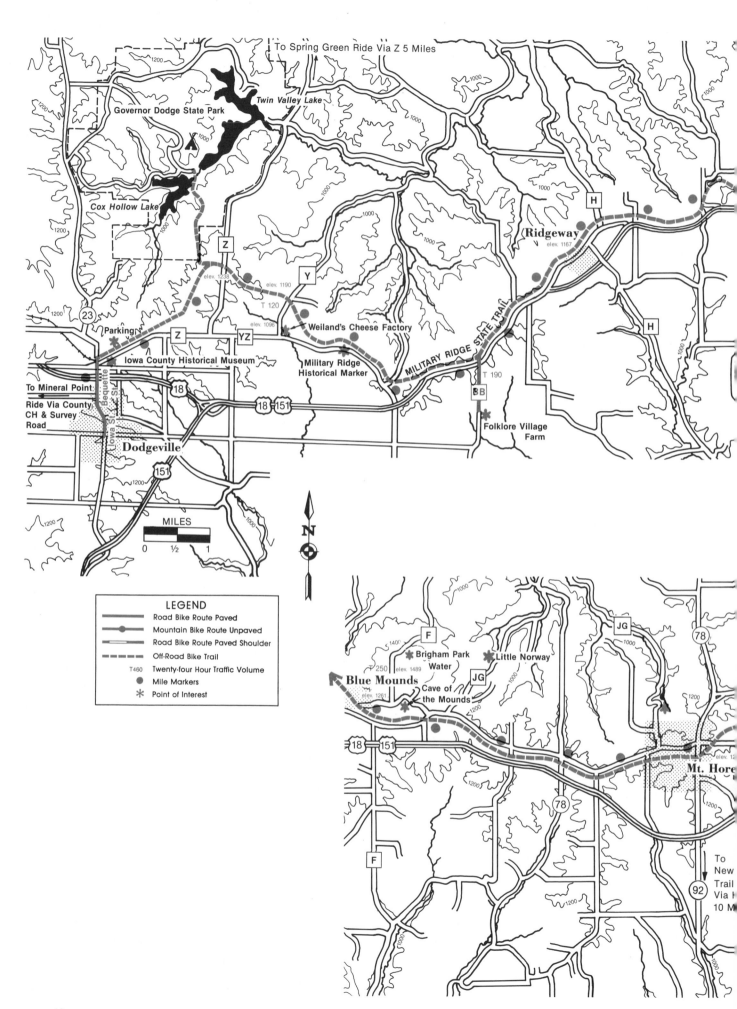

To Spring Green Ride Via Z 5 Miles

Governor Dodge State Park

Twin Valley Lake

Cox Hollow Lake

Ridgeway
elev. 1167

H

H

MILITARY RIDGE STATE TRAIL

Z
elev. 1238

Y
elev. 1190

T 120

elev. 1096

Weiland's Cheese Factory

Military Ridge
Historical Marker

T 190

BB

23

Parking

Z

Z

YZ

Iowa County Historical Museum

To Mineral Point
Ride Via County
CH & Survey
Road

Bequette

Iowa St. St.

18

Dodgeville

18 151

151

Folklore Village
Farm

MILES

0   ½   1

N

LEGEND
Road Bike Route Paved
Mountain Bike Route Unpaved
Road Bike Route Paved Shoulder
Off-Road Bike Trail
T460   Twenty-four Hour Traffic Volume
●   Mile Markers
✳   Point of Interest

F

JG

78

Brigham Park
Water

Little Norway

250
elev. 1489

JG

Blue Mounds
elev. 1261

Cave of
the Mounds

18 151

Mt. Hore

78

F

To
New
Trail
Via
92 10 M

designated them the official carbohydrate of the trail.

The Cave of the Mounds and Brigham Hearth Restaurant are a quarter mile north of the trail. The cave tour, just under an hour, will submerge you in the world of stalagtites and stalagmites. During July, the "Song of Norway" is performed each weekend in a natural amphitheatre on the grounds. Another wonderful taste of Norwegian heritage can be enjoyed at Little Norway, a cluster of sod-roofed log buildings surrounding an incredible reproduction of a StavKirke, a medieval Norse church which was hand-carved in Norway and exhibited at the Chicago World's Fair in 1893.

Folklore Village, just south of Ridgeway, is where Wisconsin's ethnic heritage comes alive. Centered around an old country schoolhouse, dancers (meaning you or anyone else who wants to join in). will step to the strains of the fiddle and accordian throughout the summer calendar of festivals and Saturday night potluck suppers. Folklore Village offers camping and youth hostel accommodations as well. For more information contact: Folklore Village Farm, Route 3, Dodgeville, WI 53533.

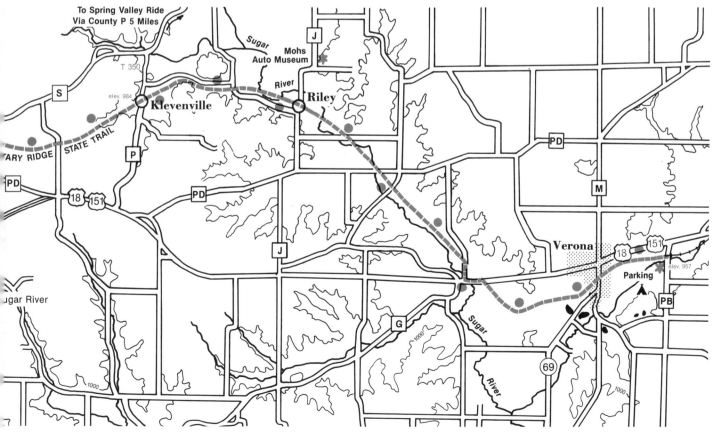

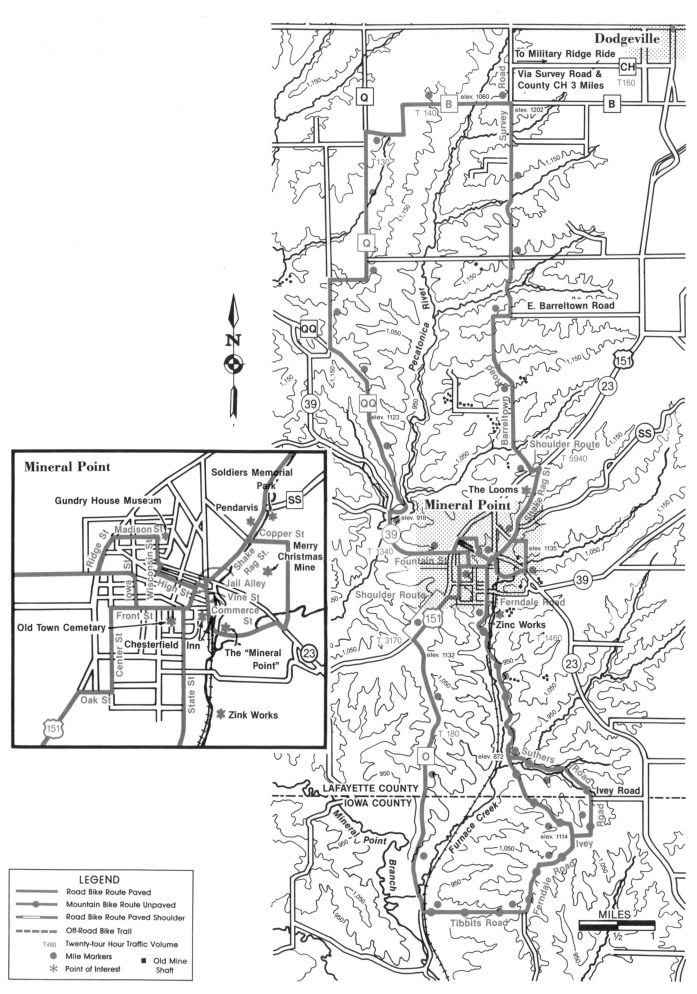

Dodgeville

To Military Ridge Ride

Via Survey Road &
County CH 3 Miles

CH

T 160

B

Q

elev. 1060

B

T 140

Survey Road

elev. 1202

1,150

T 130

1,150

1,150

1,150

E. Barreltown Road

Pecatonica River

1,050

151

23

QQ

1,150

1,150

Barreltown Road

SS

39

QQ

1,150

elev. 1123

950

1,050

1,150

Shoulder Route

T 5940

Thistle Rag St

The Looms

Mineral Point

elev. 918

39

elev. 1135

1,050

T 1340

Fountain St

Ferndale Road

39

Shoulder Route

950

Zinc Works

T 1460

151

23

T 3170

elev. 1132

950

1,050

1,050

950

T 180

Suthers Road

O

elev. 872

Ivey Road

LAFAYETTE COUNTY

IOWA COUNTY

Mineral Point

elev. 1114

Ivey

Ferndale Road

Furnace Creek

950

1,050

1,050

Branch

1,050

950

950

Tibbits Road

MILES

0   ½   1

Mineral Point (inset)

Mineral Point

Soldiers Memorial Park

Gundry House Museum

Pendarvis

SS

Madison St

Ridge St

Wisconsin St

Iowa St

High St

Copper St

Shake Rag St

Merry Christmas Mine

Jail Alley

Vine St

Commerce St

Old Town Cemetary

Front St

Center St

Chesterfield Inn

The "Mineral Point"

Oak St

State St

151

23

✳ Zink Works

LEGEND

———	Road Bike Route Paved
——●—	Mountain Bike Route Unpaved
———	Road Bike Route Paved Shoulder
- - - -	Off-Road Bike Trail
T460	Twenty-four Hour Traffic Volume
●	Mile Markers
✳	Point of Interest
■	Old Mine Shaft

MINERAL POINT RIDE

To introduce you to this unique and beautiful area, I have put together a mountain bike loop south of town, a road bike route to the north and a figure eight loop through Mineral Point's streets and alleys. You'll see unpretentious stone cottages and ornate mansions designed with skill and craftsmanship. And, if you've wondered why bicycles have such low gears, you'll find out on this tour.

Road bikers may want to take Highway 39 west out of town to County QQ. This is the valley of the Pecatonica River. As the climb begins — if you can take your eyes off the gorgeous stone farmstead nestled into the hillside — look behind you. On the crest opposite, you can see right up High Street. At one time it connected with the road you are on. The stone abutments of the old bridge still exist at the river. The quiet valleys you'll ride through once teemed with miners digging lead. When word of the 1849 California gold strike came, however, most of the miners took off. One day at the height of the exodus as many as 60 wagons heading west were lined up on High Street.

Mountain bikers may want to head south of town and wind through the lush green valley of Furnace Creek. The surface is easy-riding, crushed limestone. At the turn of the century, the largest zinc smelter in the U.S. filled this valley with the waste product of sulfuric acid production. Even 50 years after the last smelting operation nothing grows on these mounds and Furnace Creek still runs bright orange.

Farther south the route passes beautiful stone outcroppings and two farm houses constructed with the superb masonry skill of the miners and stone cutters that came here from Cornwall, England, in the 1830s. It was no accident that architect Frank Lloyd Wright chose Mineral Point Cornishman Charlie Curtis to execute many of his designs.

No matter what type of bike you have, a tour of the town is in order. The State Historical Society's Pendarvis, the restored Cornish miner cottages on Shake Rag Street, is a good place to start. The street is named for the method used by the miners' wives to call the men down from the mines for dinner, namely, shaking their dish rags out of the window. The Cornish were short-statured folk: a sub-five-foot friend found the cottages full of comforts contemporary design has deprived her of. While they used stone partly because of the lead furnace's appetite for timber, I feel that nothing could have stopped those gifted stone cutters from employing their craft to construct these charming homes. Tours of the cottages are conducted daily from May through October by the State Historical Society. A walk up the opposite hillside will take you to the site of the Merry Christmas mine shaft.

Pendarvis owes its existence to the foresight of Bob Neal and Edgar Hellum who began to preserve them in the '30s when many cottages were being destroyed. Bob passed away recently. He endowed the Public Library on High Street with his remarkable collection of books and maps, which a rare books dealer helped him accumulate. This treasure is now kept in a special Mineral Point room.

Further east on Shake Rag is the old Mineral Springs Brewery building. Today it is The Looms, a weaving studio and museum, exemplifying the arts and crafts community that has found such hospitable surroundings in Mineral Point. Originally the building had a stone tower at each end. In 1878 a tornado destroyed the south tower. For years afterwards, the brewery marketed Tornado Beer.

For a real taste of the town's past, stop by the Chesterfield Inn on Commerce Street for their daily special, Cornish pasty. This traditional meat and potato pie is nothing fancy, but it has never failed to put a smile on a miner's or bicyclist's face. You can sample other Cornish treats and ice cream and even enjoy a bed-and-breakfast experience in the historic atmosphere of one of Mineral Point's oldest hostels.

On High Street you will notice a statue of a dog projecting over a store front. This was the symbol of the Gundry and Gray Dry Goods store. Gundry came from Cornwall and his Victorian mansion is now the Gundry House Museum, housing a remarkable collection of minerals. The extensive grounds are an arboretum. Gundry planted many exotic trees and he also preserved one of the great prairie oaks that now takes three people to reach around.

If you would like to delve further into the past, a detailed guide to the architecture and history of the town is available at many locations. You will find, however, that the vitality of Mineral Point is not all in the past. Today's artists and craftpersons continue to create humble objects of intrinsic value, made traditionally with pride and care.

My mother joined me on my latest visit to Mineral Point. As we crossed High Street, where stone store fronts are two stories high on the street and four stories high in the back, she said, "Why here comes George Branger. I'll bet he's been the mayor for 20 years." George soon corrected her misconception. His 83rd birthday marks his 23rd term as mayor.

When I asked his secret, he said he had a rare immunity to the slings and arrows that bring down so many politicians. "I'm not in business, so if people don't like what I say or do, I can't be boycotted. I don't have many relatives to pressure me and I have hardly any friends."

Few people take themselves too seriously in Mineral Point.

LEGEND

─────	Road Bike Route Paved
──●──	Mountain Bike Route Unpaved
──▭──	Road Bike Route Paved Shoulder
─ ─ ─	Off-Road Bike Trail
T460	Twenty-four Hour Traffic Volume
●	Mile Markers
✳	Point of Interest

SPRING GREEN RIDE

On the maps it's Jones Valley. But to Frank Lloyd Wright and his Welsh pioneer forebears, it was simply "the valley."

Looking out from Aldebaran you can appreciate the reverence that many feel for this place. This is the farm where Wright spent his boyhood summers, "adding tired to tired" working with his uncle. You can imagine the impression the view made on the boy a hundred years ago. It was this natural beauty, the buff-colored limestone outcroppings, that inspired Wright to create architecture that existed in harmony with its surroundings.

Wright's mother fixed upon architecture as the career for her son even before he was born, filling his nursery with wood-cut prints of English cathedrals. Yet her unsuccessful marriage to Wright's father and subsequent poverty had an even greater effect on his future. Architecture school was out of the question. He enrolled in engineering at the University of Wisconsin where, Wright would one day note, he was "spared the curse of . . . architectural education." A few years later at the age of 18, he arrived in Chicago with $7 in his pocket and the knowledge that the foundation of conventional architecture was set in the sands of pretension and fashion. In 1909, 22 years later, after creating a new architectural style and scandalizing Chicago with his personal life, Wright returned to the valley for good. Ostracized and ignored, but unbowed, he built Taliesin "of the hill" rather than on it and rebuilt it twice after disastrous fires. His innovations were innumerable and included the currently in vogue atrium and earth-sheltered passive solar designs. When Frank Lloyd Wright died in 1959, he was the most prolific architect in the history of the world. His grave in the small cemetery at Unity Chapel is marked by a stone ring and plain balanced limestone monolith that seems symbolic of his Celtic heritage and ancient Welsh family motto: "Truth Against the World."

Appropriately, the valley is a showcase of Wright's work. His legacy lives on in the Taliesin Fellowship. You can tour their studios at Hillside School from June through mid-September. Use extra caution on Highway 23 south of the river as the traffic is heavy. The little park at Peck's Landing at the north end of the Highway 23 bridge offers a fine view of the Spring Green Restaurant where you can enjoy a meal or a drink overlooking the river in the wonderful atmosphere of this Wright-designed structure.

Upper Snead Creek and Percussion Rock roads are two of the most beautiful in the state, although the view of the magnificent green, lichen-covered spires of Percussion Rock requires a tough climb. House on the Rock is an interesting attraction that unfortunately cannot be approached from any roads I can recommend for bicycling. The original structure envelops one of the many free standing pillar rocks of the area, and has been added to over the years. The complex now includes museums, amusements and shops, featuring the work of local craftspeople. Farther north on Highway 23 stands a Wright-designed country schoolhouse and the Wyoming Cheese Factory, where fresh cheese curds should not be missed.

If steep hills are not your thing, you can enjoy a nearly flat loop along County C and Kennedy Road where you'll be treated to some beautiful views of the Wisconsin River, a pleasant stop at Florence Laudon Park and a visit to Spring Green. There you will find a gorgeous oval limestone bank building designed by the Taliesin Fellowship. If you have worked up an appetite, there is a bakery; I also recommend visiting the Prairieland Cafe, located in a corner of the General Store.

Mountain bikers can, for a nominal fee, obtain a map at the Spring Green Restaurant and take advantage of the Wintergreen cross-country ski trails for an exciting off-road ride that features ridgetop views of the valley and river. The trails are wide with a firm surface and are well marked with trail name arrows.

For a farther-ranging mountain bike ride, try Lakeview and Snead Creek roads, which will lead you to the unincorporated town of Blue Grass where a big green reflective sign proclaims the town's population—11. You won't find much there, but if you get as far as the Pleasant Ridge store, you'll be treated to basic merchandising—no credit cards please.

Accommodations are available at several Spring Green motels. Small groups can stay at Aldebaran (inquire at the Spring Green Restaurant), the redesigned farm complex once belonging to Frank Lloyd Wright's uncle, or at Wildwood Studios located in a quiet valley nook. A number of camping options exist. You can reach a special bicycle campground in Governor Dodge State Park by taking County Z to the Military Ridge State Trail. Privately operated Spring Valley Campgrounds also offers Youth Hostel accommodations. You can camp at Tower Hill State Park and visit the reconstructed shot tower where lead was made into buckshot in the years before Wisconsin was a territory.

July through October, you can top off your visit by attending a matinee or evening performance of Shakespeare in a beautiful, natural amphitheater. The American Players acting troupe is one of Wisconsin's cultural treasures; you can picnic on their grounds.

Those attracted to multi-function bike tripping might want to consider a combined bicycle/canoe outing. You can lock your bikes at the boat landing near Lone Rock, put in or rent a canoe at Bob's Riverside near Spring Green, and enjoy the beauty of the river from both land and water.

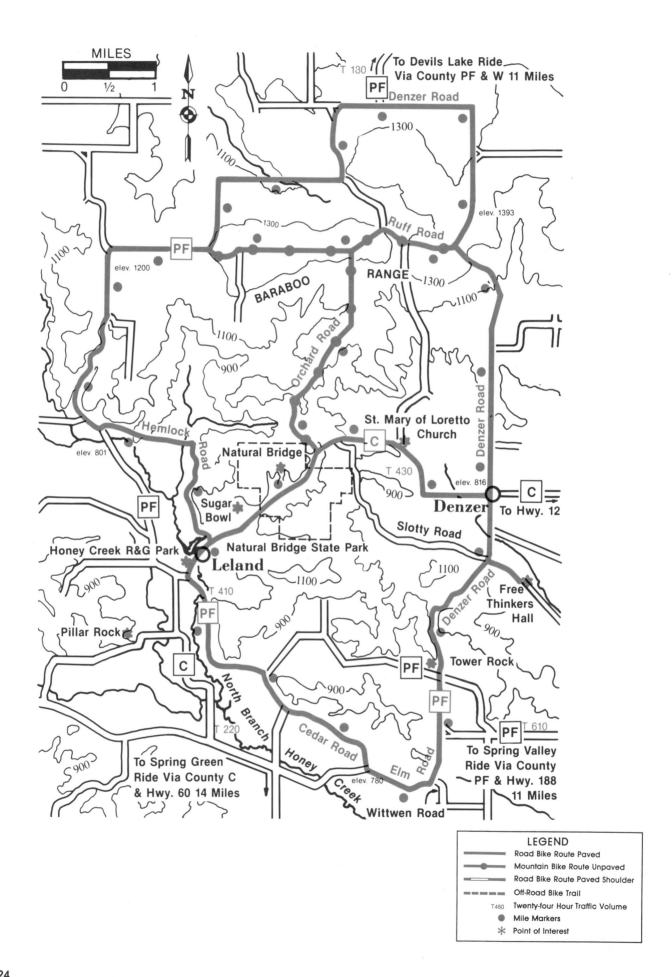

MILES

0   ½   1

N

To Devils Lake Ride
Via County PF & W 11 Miles

T 130

PF Denzer Road

1300

elev. 1393

1100

Ruff Road

1300

1300

1100

PF

elev. 1200

BARABOO   RANGE

1100

Orchard Road

1100

900

St. Mary of Loretto
Church

Denzer Road

C

T 430

Hemlock

elev. 801

Natural Bridge

Road

900

elev. 816

PF

Sugar
Bowl

Denzer   C

To Hwy. 12

Natural Bridge State Park

Slotty Road

Honey Creek R&G Park

Leland

1100

1100

T 410

900

Free
Thinkers
Hall

PF

Denzer Road

900

Pillar Rock

C

Tower Rock

900

PF

T 220

North Branch

900

900

PF

Cedar Road

PF T 610

To Spring Green
Ride Via County C
& Hwy. 60 14 Miles

900

Honey

Elm Road

To Spring Valley
Ride Via County
PF & Hwy. 188
11 Miles

Creek

elev. 780

Wittwen Road

LEGEND

Road Bike Route Paved

Mountain Bike Route Unpaved

Road Bike Route Paved Shoulder

Off-Road Bike Trail

T460   Twenty-four Hour Traffic Volume

Mile Markers

* Point of Interest

NATURAL BRIDGE STATE PARK RIDE

Natural Bridge, one of the state's most interesting geological features, is also the site of Wisconsin's oldest-known human habitation. This narrow, four-foot-wide arch of sandstone 25 feet above the floor of the gorge is tucked in an out-of-the-way cleft along the southwestern edge of the imposing Baraboo Range.

Ten thousand years ago, it was the autumn home of bands of nomadic hunters who lived off white-tailed deer, which are still abundant today. An anthropologist could point out a number of logical reasons why these people chose to return to the rock shelter for a millenium. The visitor, unencumbered by scientific constraints, will recognize the spiritual nature of the place.

In the last century, the flat sandy floor beneath the arch and its cool shelter of overhanging rock was a popular place for picnics and dances. Today it is preserved as one of our newest state parks. A wonderful nature trail identifies trees and plants and explains how the Indians used them.

Appropriately, your visit to Natural Bridge will be on foot, but there is plenty of great bicycling to be enjoyed. The long on-road route will take you 22 miles and 600 feet to the top of the Baraboo Range. You can cut that distance in half and reduce the hills to one gradual 200-footer by sticking to the southern loop. You will miss the grand overview of the north range and the thrilling downhill runs, but the beauty of the valley just about makes up for it. The route is punctuated by towering wooded hills with bright sandstone outcroppings. These take on grand forms at tower rock, pillar rock and sugar bowl. The roadside is lined with pioneer buildings and 19th century farmsteads—the ride becomes a tour around numerous examples of simple, sturdy craftsmanship and architectural styles of bygone days. One remarkable sandstone structure, the subject of calendar photos, is St. Mary of Loretto Church, which sits quietly along County C against the green background of the Baraboo Range.

As you cross Honey Creek south of Denzer, you will spot a singular grove of white pines to the southeast. This majestic stand shelters the Freethinkers Hall and Cemetery. The unpretentious white clapboard building is a remnant of the Free Thought movement or "Freie Gemeinde," an anti-clerical society that had currency among the German settlers who populated the valley. They studied the works of Thomas Paine, one of their heroes, and Charles Darwin. An excellent library of the movement exists at the still-active Free Thought Hall in nearby Sauk City. The pines were planted in 1866. In case the peaceful spot appeals to you as a potential final resting place, I should mention that this is the only cemetery in the U.S. where you have to be a freethinker to qualify.

If your appetite for refreshment extends beyond beer and bar snacks, bring a picnic lunch, as all you will find in the neat crossroad villages of Leland and Denzer are taverns. These typical rural Wisconsin watering holes have their appeal, however, and I particularly enjoyed Goerk's in Denzer and Sprecher's in Leland.

Mountain bike riders will find Orchard and Ruff roads custom-made, or rather I should say preserved, for their enjoyment. The designation of the narrow, picturesque trails as Rustic Roads means their character is protected from change or development. They are more than just charming routes from point to point. They have an intrinsic beauty all of their own.

Pioneer buildings and 19th century farmsteads line this picturesque route.

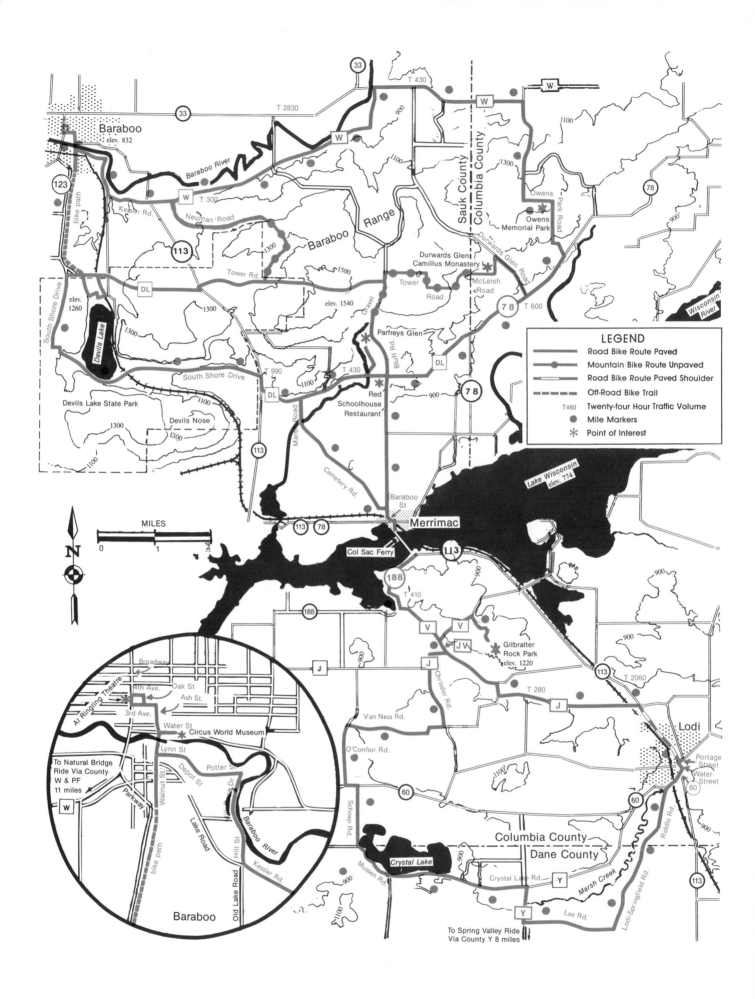

LEGEND

———————	Road Bike Route Paved
——●——●——	Mountain Bike Route Unpaved
———————	Road Bike Route Paved Shoulder
– – – – –	Off-Road Bike Trail
T460	Twenty-four Hour Traffic Volume
●	Mile Markers
✳	Point of Interest

Baraboo
elev. 832

Baraboo River

Baraboo Range

Sauk County
Columbia County

Owens
Memorial Park

Durwards Glen
Camillus Monastery

McLeish
Road

Kessler Rd.

Neuman Road

Tower Rd.

elev. 1260

Devils Lake

South Shore Drive

Devils Lake State Park

Devils Nose

elev. 1540

Tower Road

Gravel

Parfreys Glen

Bluff Rd.

Red
Schoolhouse
Restaurant

Marsh Road

Cemetery Rd.

Baraboo
St

Lake Wisconsin
elev. 774

Merrimac

Col Sac Ferry

Wisconsin River

Gilbralter
Rock Park
elev. 1220

Van Ness Rd.

Chrissler Rd.

O'Connor Rd.

Lodi

Portage
Street
Water Street

Columbia County
Dane County

Crystal Lake

Crystal Lake Rd.

Mussen Rd.

Schoep Rd.

Marsh Creek

Lodi-Springfield Rd.

Lee Rd.

Riddle Rd.

To Spring Valley Ride
Via County Y 8 miles

MILES
0   1   2

N

Baraboo

Broadway

4th Ave.
Oak St.
Ash St.

Al Ringling Theatre

3rd Ave.

Water St.   Circus World Museum

Lynn St.

To Natural Bridge
Ride Via County
W & PF
11 miles

Parkway

Walnut St.

Depot St.

Potter St.

Hill St.

Lake Road

Old Lake Road

Kessler Rd.

Baraboo River

bike path

Roads and route numbers: 33, T 2830, T 430, W, 900, 1100, 1300, 78, 1100, Park Road, Owens, Durwards Glen Road, T 600, 113, 123, bike path, DL, 1300, 1500, 1300, 1300, T 990, T 430, DL, DL, 1100, 1100, 900, 78, 1100, 113, 78, 113, 188, T 410, 188, V, V, JV, J, J, J, 60, 113, T 280, T 2060, 60, 900, 900, Y, Y, 113, 900

26

DEVILS LAKE RIDE

Devils Lake State Park is the most popular park in Wisconsin. This might seem like a good reason to stay away, but keep in mind that the appeal lies in the fact that there is such great beauty here. If you can let it soak in for even a second you will come away a different person. There are many times during the riding season when the park is not crowded, and there is always an abundance of lightly trafficked roads to enjoy in the area. The ban on motorboats makes the lake a wonderful spot for swimming, snorkeling, canoeing and sail boarding.

The Baraboo Range, which is the name for the towering bright quartzite bluffs that cradle Devils Lake, has been called a geographical fossil. Technically the range is a pre-Cambrian monadanock, the remnant core of an ancient mountain range that was completely submerged beneath the ocean; it is now reemerging from layers of sedimentary sandstone laid down by the sea. As you strain to the top of these rugged 500 foot bluffs, keep in mind that the remaining sandstone makes them only half as tall as their pre-deluge height.

The gap in the Baraboo Range where the lake lies was once the course of the Wisconsin River. During the last glacial epoch, ice sheets pushed into the gap from the north and the east, forcing the Wisconsin River to flow along its present course and leaving the basin which became Devils Lake.

The long climbs and thrilling descents to be found in the Baraboo Range are memorable, with fantastic views of the river valley along Tower Road and at Owens Memorial Park. For easier riding take the free Col Sac ferry at Merrimac and cruise the beautiful roads between Crystal Lake and Lodi. You can savor an ice cream cone while waiting, but you won't be waiting long. No matter how crowded the ferry is there is always room for a bicycle.

Lodi is a pleasant stop, as you might imagine. Any place that has the audacity to erect signs that proudly proclaim "Lodi, Home of Suzi the Duck" must have something to offer. I have enjoyed Curley's Cafe and the bakery across the street, as well as that classic bicyclist's oasis, the root beer stand. Where the creek passes under the main street you can buy a handful of corn from an old coin-op bubble gum machine to toss to the ducks below, one of which might be the real Suzi.

If the moderate hills around Lodi have gotten your courage up, you might want to take on Gilbralter Rock, a beautiful cliff of St. Peters sandstone topped with a county park. The view from the top is spectacular. You can see as far as Blue Mounds, but you will pay for it as the climb up the road is one of the toughest I have found. Back on the north side of the river be sure to visit Parfrey's Glen. This enchanting spot is a state scientific area, which harbors rare plant communities within its cool, deep-shaded chasm. I find myself unconsciously speaking in subdued tones out of an overwhelming feeling of reverence. Nearby you will find the Red Schoolhouse Restaurant, situated in its namesake, and a nice sandwich menu. This is your only dining choice north of the ferry and east of Devils Lake.

No visit to the area would be complete without a trip to Baraboo and a stop at Circus World Museum. Baraboo is the hometown of the Ringling Brothers and the museum tells their story as well as those of other circuses from around the country. These local boys came a long way from the day a hundred years ago when they hit the road in a handful of farm wagons with a dog act and a blind hyena. The height of the circus was in the 1940s when "The Greatest Show on Earth" traveled in a hundred, double-long railroad cars with 50 elephants and a big top that covered the area of two football fields. The history of all this is preserved by the museum along with dozens of beautifully restored, colorful hand-carved circus wagons. But most significantly, Circus World is a living museum with clowns, animals and daring performers. Although you have to go *to* the circus, rather than the other way around, you still cannot help but join the excitement.

Stop at Devil's Lake for more motorless relaxation, such as swimming, snorkeling, and even sailing.

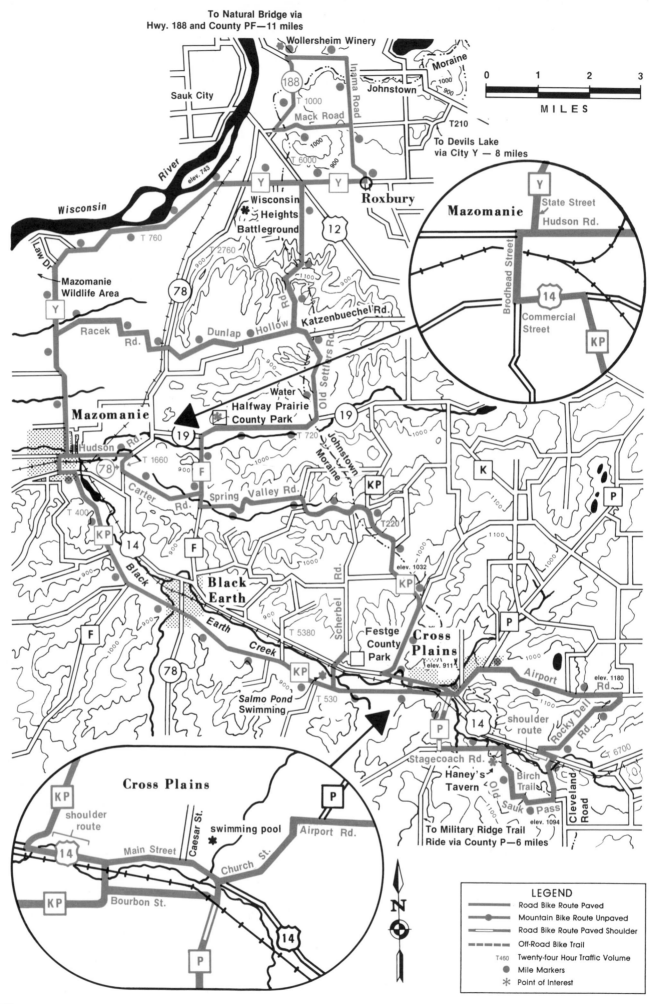

To Natural Bridge via
Hwy. 188 and County PF—11 miles

Wollersheim Winery

Moraine

Johnstown

Sauk City

0 1 2 3
MILES

River

Wisconsin

188
T 1000

Mack Road

Inama Road

1000
900

T210

To Devils Lake
via City Y — 8 miles

T 6000

900

Y   Y

Roxbury

Mazomanie

Y
State Street
Hudson Rd.

Wisconsin
Heights
Battleground

12

Brodhead Street

elev. 743

T 760

900 T 2760

Mazomanie
Wildlife Area

78

1100

14

Commercial
Street

KP

Y

Racek
Rd.

Dunlap Hollow
Rd.

Katzenbuechel Rd.

Old Settlers Rd.

Water
Halfway Prairie
County Park

19

K

P

Mazomanie

19

T 720

Johnstown
Moraine

1000

KP

Hudson Rd.

78

T 1660

F

Spring Valley Rd.

T220

elev. 1032

1100

Carter   Rd.

1000

900

KP

T 400

14

F

1000

900

Black
Earth

Black   Earth   Creek

Scherbel Rd.

1000

KP

1100

P

F

78

T 5380

Festge
County
Park

Cross
Plains

elev. 911

Airport

elev. 1180

1000

Rocky Dell Rd.

900

KP

T 530

Salmo Pond
Swimming

P

14

shoulder
route

1100

T 6700

Cross Plains

KP

shoulder
route

KP

14

Main Street

Caesar St.

swimming pool

Airport Rd.

Church St.

Bourbon St.

14

P

Stagecoach Rd.

Haney's
Tavern

Birch
Trail

Old Sauk Pass

Cleveland Road

elev. 1094

To Military Ridge Trail
Ride via County P—6 miles

N

LEGEND
———— Road Bike Route Paved
—●— Mountain Bike Route Unpaved
═══ Road Bike Route Paved Shoulder
- - - Off-Road Bike Trail
T460 Twenty-four Hour Traffic Volume
● Mile Markers
✻ Point of Interest

28

SPRING VALLEY RIDE

Spring Valley is the end: the end, that is, of the advance of the glacial ice sheet. You can stand at the corner of Spring Valley and Scherbel roads and see very plainly where it stopped. Looking to the east, you will notice the hills that form the valley sides are rounded and their smooth surfaces have lent themselves to farming. These are part of the Johnstown Moraine, the glacier's last bit of handiwork before the big meltdown. In contrast, the valley sides around the intersection and to the west remain steep and rugged, with unmolested angular blocks of stone protruding from the slopes; agriculture is confined to the bottomland.

The beauty of the valleys on this tour is enhanced by a rich history. If you find the story of the glacier a bit dry, a visit to the Wollersheim Winery may be more refreshing. At the impressive limestone winery, a masterpiece of the masonry skill German settlers brought to this area, you can taste history by sampling the product of the vine. The vineyard is in its third, and finally successful, incarnation under the Wollersheim management.

During the last half of the 19th century, it was operated by Peter Kehl who had the present buildings constructed. He purchased the land from Agoston Haraszthy, an ill-fated Hungarian Count who had been cast into the New World by the machinations of court intrigue. The Count's European vines failed to survive one of the harshest Wisconsin winters ever, and he ventured off to California. There, the poor quality of the mission grape wine and the seemingly ideal climate for vinticulture motivated him to persuade the state legislature to sponsor a vine-buying expedition to Europe. Alas, when Haraszthy returned with 100,000 cuttings, he found that the Civil War had wrought profound changes, one of which was the refusal of the new regime to reimburse him for his expenses. As a result of his efforts, he is today revered as the father of the California wine industry. At the time however, he was forced to auction off the vines at a fraction of their value. Seeking new opportunities with the money he had salvaged, the unlucky man was last seen crossing an alligator-infested river in Nicaragua. After tasting the delicious Wollersheim wine you will probably agree that the Count should have stayed in Wisconsin and given it another try.

The German architectural influence extends throughout the northern part of this tour. At the crossroads town of Roxbury you will find its manifestation in the impressive construction of St. Norberts Church. This is balanced, across the street, by the German hospitality waiting for you at the Gasthaus and Dorfhaus. The former is an architectural treasure and a pleasant place to stop for a burger and a beer. The latter is a supper club with an all-you-can-eat Friday night fish fry that will commit you to a mega-mile weekend of bicycling:

West of Roxbury, just southeast of the intersection of County Y and Highway 78, is the site of the Wisconsin Heights Battleground. On July 21, 1832, the aging Sauk chief, Black Hawk, and about 50 braves held off the vastly superior U.S. Army while their women and children escaped across the Wisconsin River. The British Band, as they were called for having taken the English side in the War of 1812, made it to the Mississippi before they were annihilated.

The eastern press had a heyday with the war. The captured Black Hawk was taken through major coastal cities calling the attention of the nation to Wisconsin, where the Indians had been subdued . On meeting President Andrew Jackson, Black Hawk pointed out that if he had had an army as massive as Jackson's, the president would be his prisoner. The old chief's observation that he was no longer a threat because he had no people to lead impressed Jackson, who had a reputation as an Indian fighter. Black Hawk was released to spend his remaining years in peace.

If your pedaling brings you to the southern end of the tour loops, you are probably ready for refreshment. If there is a picnic lunch in your bike bag, Festge County Park is the ideal spot to stop and enjoy it. The overview of the valley from the edge of the park is a postcard-perfect picture of rural Wisconsin. You can also take a dip in Salmo Pond, a popular swimming hole on the south side of the highway. You had better have packed a lunch if you visit Haney's Tavern on Stagecoach Road. The historic structure is one of the oldest buildings in Dane County, but is today a private residence. Haney's tradition of providing relief to the weary traveler has been assumed in Cross Plains by Sheldon's Restaurant on Main Street. Their homemade soups have a reputation for reviving tired bicyclists.

Try Wollersheim Winery's latest vintage and tour their 125-year-old stone buildings, which overlook the Wisconsin River.

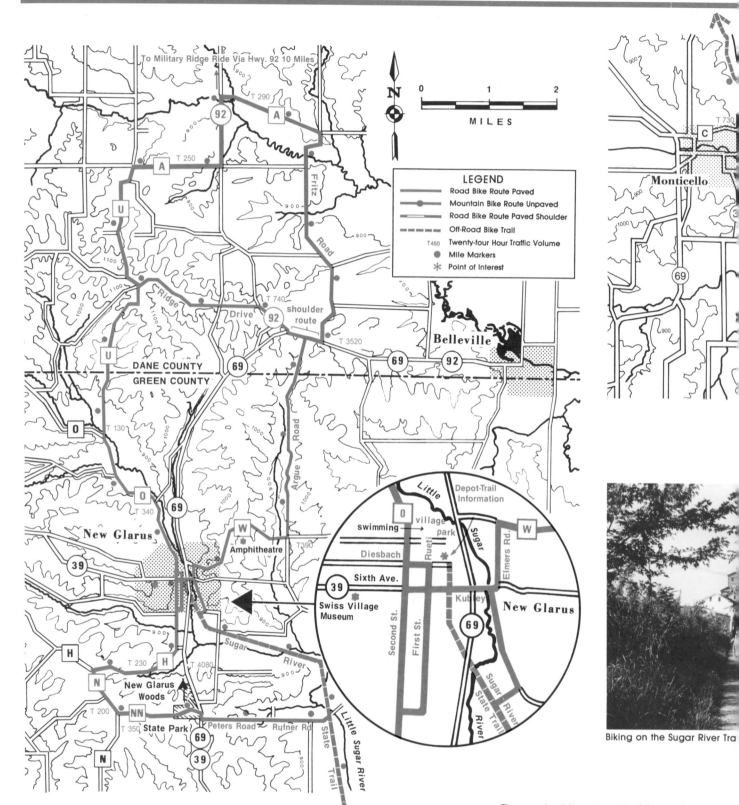

Biking on the Sugar River Tra[il]

During the ten years since the opening of the Sugar River State Trail, New Glarus has fallen in love with bicycling and bicyclists have fallen in love with New Glarus. The small town, known as Wisconsin's little Switzerland, has a hospitable Swiss spirit that's as common as the town's chalet-like architecture. Dinner on the porch of the New Glarus Hotel, a glass of Wisconsin-brewed beer at the

Glarner Stube or a sample of the uncarboconscious offerings of the New Glarus Bakery will make that clear. Some residents still speak Glarnese German, a purer version, it was discovered a few years ago, than that spoken in Switzerland today.

The Sugar River Trail follows an old railroad bed that winds south among the lovely meanders of its namesake river.

The crushed limestone trail has only a three percent grade, and suits tenspeeds, mountain bikes, and riders of all abilities. Much of the surrounding land is a wildlife area, and your ride may be highlighted by sightings of hawks and migratory waterfowl, which visit the river's marshy backwaters. You'll enjoy a grand overview of the river valley from the little county park on Park Road. The pleasant towns of Monticello, Albany and Brodhead lie strung out along the trail at

NEW GLARUS/SUGAR RIVER TRAIL RIDE

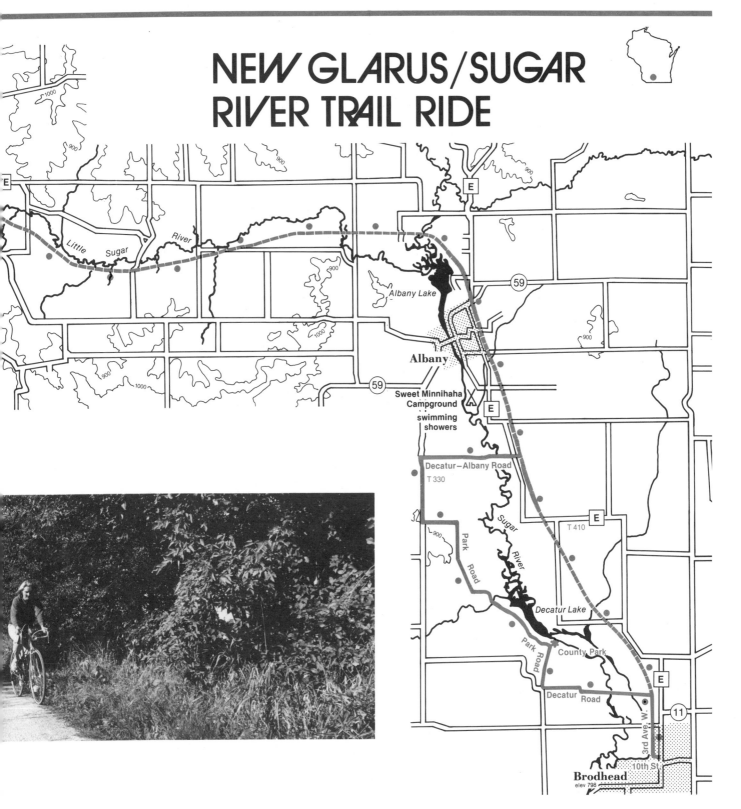

intervals that seem to accommodate a bicyclist's thirst on a hot summer day. If you make it all the way to Brodhead, the old hotel there is known to set a fine table. You can camp at Albany, or at New Glarus Woods State Park.

If you'd like to take your ten-speed out for a hilly bicycling experience, the New Glarus area offers many quiet, scenic roads, ideal if you like a good long climb. Once you have made it to the top, you're rewarded with scenic overviews.

Riding along Ridge Drive, you can see Blue Mounds on the horizon 16 miles to the northwest. If you return to New Glarus via County W, you'll crest a hill and be greeted with a bird's-eye view.

Should you happen to be visiting on the last weekend of June or on Labor Day weekend, you can enjoy the townspeople's production of "Heidi" and "Wilhelm Tell," respectively, in a beautiful natural amphitheater in the woods just south of County W. The New Glarners go all out

to bring to life these famous stories from their homeland. If your thirst for Swiss culture has not been fully quenched, you'll usually find an outstanding polka band on festival weekends oom-pah-pahing at Puempels Tavern on Kubley Street. I recommend training for the event, however. After being dragged onto the dance floor and suffering cramps in five different places, I realized that being fit for bicycling and fit for polkaing are two different things.

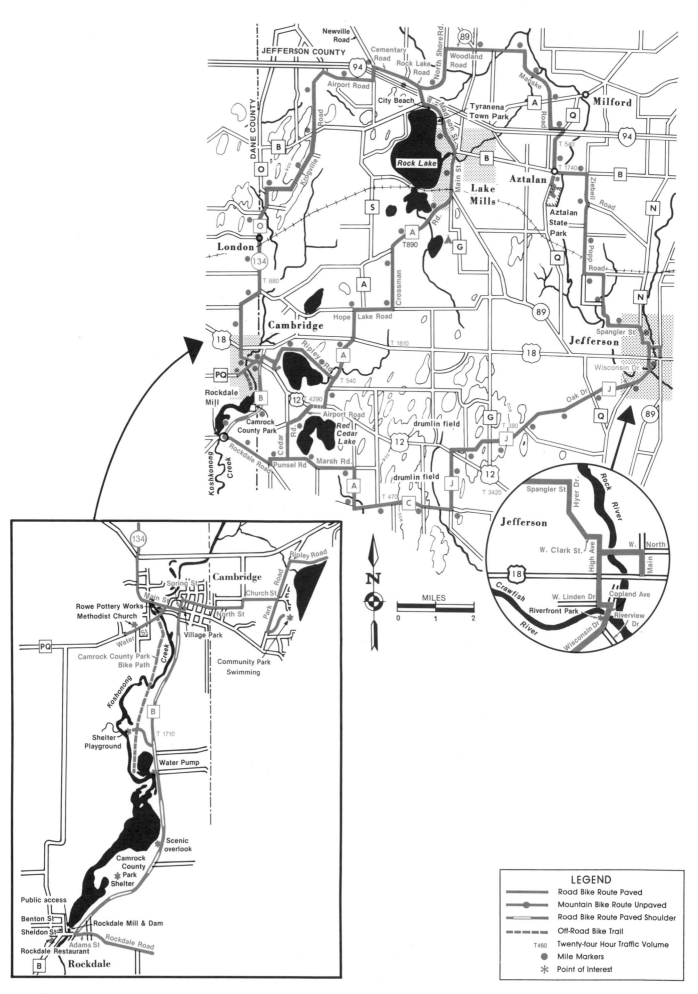

AZTALAN RIDE

The Cambridge Bakery is a perfect stop for hungry bicyclists.

Aztalan is Wisconsin's most significant prehistoric archeological site. Long ago, the stockaded village on the banks of the Crawfish River was the northernmost outpost of the Middle Mississippian culture whose vast trade network dominated mid-America. The settlement disappeared years before Columbus found the New World. Excavation at Cahokia, the culture's center near East St. Louis, have revealed a fortified city of 40,000 to 100,00 residents. The history of the Indians is one of tremendous diversity, and as you walk over the grassy, pyramid-shaped mounds at Aztalan, you may well wonder about the stories buried here.

You'll find the pedaling easy along these lightly traveled roads rolling through the marshes and rich farmland. Big herds of Holsteins indicate the importance of dairy farming. Although modern farm operations are highly mechanized, there is one crop that still involves a great amount of handwork. Tobacco growing—for cigar wrappers and chewing—puts hard cash in the farmer's pockets in February. In September, you can see families in the fields, giving the crop the careful handling it requires at harvest.

Prosperous farms make for pleasant and comfortable small towns. While the feed mill is always a focus, there are other amenities. On Main Street in Lake Mills, the Pyramid Cafe has been a popular gathering place for local cyclists. Cambridge has a bakery that has kept me in carbohydrates for years. Just down the street in the old blacksmith's shop is the showroom of Rowe Pottery Works. This local company handcrafts exquisite salt-glazed pottery embellished with early American motifs. I think you will find a stop at the Rockdale Restaurant for breakfast or lunch a cultural as well as culinary adventure. The small cafe occupies a corner of an old cream brick building. It serves hearty home-cooked breakfasts and lunches to farm and mill hands. The conversation usually has an agri-focus. The first thing you learn about farming in a place like this is that it's too dry, too wet, too hot or too cold. And if it's not, it's going to be.

Rockdale is a picturesque little village built around a 130-year-old mill and dam. The mill pond backs up for miles and creates the marshland that is Cam-Rock County Park. Marshes are normally impenetrable, but you have a unique opportunity to explore this one. Perhaps you'll glimpse a muskrat, beaver or the shy great blue heron from a partially completed railroad grade bike path that goes halfway between Cambridge and Rockdale. Keep your eyes on the trail though; the path ends abruptly at Koshkonong Creek (the bridge awaits funding) and there are no warning signs. The park is a great place to take young children on a bicycle adventure. There is a shelter and playground midway and the paved shoulders on County B make for a comfortable on-road ride. If the weather is hot, you'll find the clean waters of Lake Ripley or Rock Lake refreshing. City Beach in Lake Mills is free, and the Community Park charges a nominal fee.

The Koshkonong valley has a distinct Scandinavian character. In the 19th century, the largest Norwegian settlement in the country occupied the surrounding prairie land. On Water Street in Cambridge stands the oldest Scandinavian Methodist Church in the world. The beautiful little stone structure is visible as you ride north on the bike path. The newly arrived, mostly Lutheran, Norwegian immigrants, once out from under the rigid control of old country instutitions, had a great deal to say about their method of worship, and they didn't always agree with each other. South of Rockdale, there are two Lutheran churches just a hundred yards apart. They are the result of a theological schism that in the 1880s split the congregation. Today, the two hold services together, using each church on alternate Sundays.

The area also has an interesting geological history. The elongated hills that County J and Kroghville Road wind through are drumlins created by the last glacier. Their prevailing northeast-southwest orientation is evidence that the powerful ice sheets flowed that way. As you tour through the area, it will be no surprise that both prehistoric and present day peoples found it a pleasant place to live.

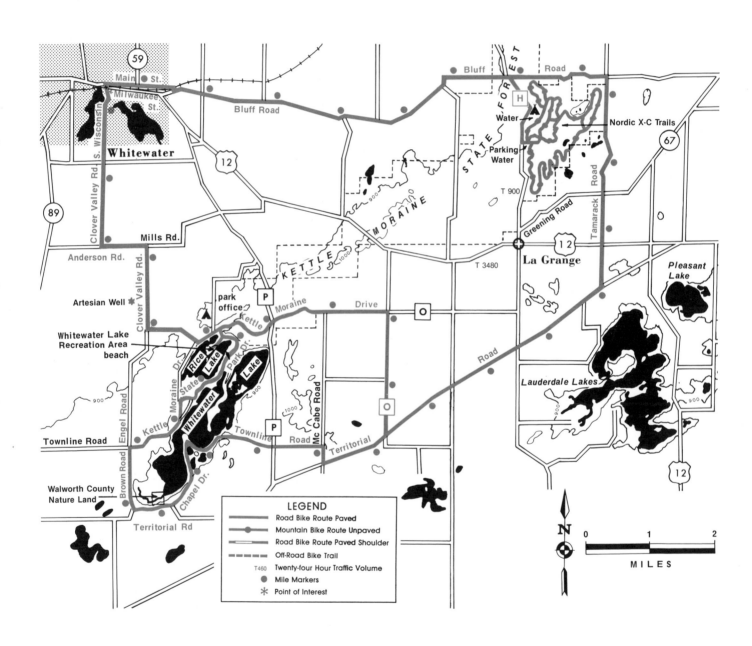

LEGEND

———	Road Bike Route Paved
—•—	Mountain Bike Route Unpaved
▭	Road Bike Route Paved Shoulder
– – –	Off-Road Bike Trail
T460	Twenty-four Hour Traffic Volume
●	Mile Markers
✳	Point of Interest

59
Main St.
Milwaukee St.
S. Wisconsin
Whitewater
89
Clover Valley Rd. S.
Mills Rd.
Anderson Rd.
12
Bluff Road
Bluff Road
Bluff Road
H
Water
Parking Water
Nordic X-C Trails
67
KETTLE MORAINE STATE FOREST
T 900
Greening Road
12
La Grange
Tamarack Road
T 3480
Pleasant Lake
Artesian Well ✳
Clover Valley Rd.
park office
P
Kettle Moraine Drive
O
O
Road
Whitewater Lake Recreation Area beach
Rice Lake
Park Dr.
Whitewater Lake
Kettle Moraine State Dr.
900
1000
McCabe Road
Lauderdale Lakes
900
900
Engel Road
Brown Road
Townline Road
Townline Road
Territorial Road
P
Territorial
12
Walworth County Nature Land
Chapel Dr.
Territorial Rd.

N

0   1   2

MILES

SOUTHERN KETTLE MORAINE RIDE

Bicycling in the southeastern part of the state is so easy that you may find yourself looking for some hills. If so, head to the rolling terrain of the Kettle Moraine State Forest.

The hills mark the juncture of two great glacial lobes. The larger one to the east carved Lake Michigan while the other created Green Bay, Lake Winnebago and the Horicon Marsh. Along the line where the lobes met, earth and rock were ground together with chunks of ice. Eventually the huge ice sheets melted, creating the surrounding flat outwash plains. When the ice blocks buried in the hills also melted, the land was left pockmarked with depressions, called kettles, which give the area its name.

When I discovered that two old friends would be back in Wisconsin for early September bike riding, I immediately decided my on-road route through the Southern Kettle Moraine State Forest would be perfect for a nostalgic tour. I had already mountain-biked the area's nordic ski trails. Well-marked and great fun, they dip in and out of the kettle depressions. (The trails should be avoided on fall color weekends, however, when hikers appear in throngs.)

On the appointed day, Karen, who was visiting from San Francisco, and Lew, who had been abroad in American Samoa, and I found ourselves rolling along the brick streets past the Victorian buildings of Whitewater, anxious to hit the open road. The flat farmland and vast horizon along Bluff Road contrasted sharply with Karen's Bay area hills and Lew's island confines. When I noticed that County H had been widened, we decided to turn south on it. We had a pleasant stop at the campground to fill our water bottles from the hand pump, but the increased traffic on the improved road forced us to admit Tamarack Road would have been a better choice.

Winding around the developed southern end of Whitewater Lake, we stopped for a while at Walworth County Natureland. The park lived up to its name. A pure spring bubbled up from beneath the roots of an ancient tree, and farther down, where it flowed into the lake, we sat and watched a mallard herd her ducklings while a muskrat scurried among the watercress and a heron swooped in for a brief visit.

Back on the road, we turned a corner and started up a steep hill. Lew found himself first in the wrong gear and then on the ground, laughing. Used to pedaling around Samoa in sandals, he had forgotten the consequences of being strapped into toe clips. A little later, a big roadside Pabst sign was a signal to Lew: the rural Wisconsin bicycling experience he had been looking for was at hand. We carefully negotiated the steep drive down to a lakeside establishment, but when we ordered three cold beers, we discovered that the sign was out of date. Whitewater Lake had gone dry.

Back in Whitewater, we found ourselves at a different type of watering hole. The Circle Tap seemed most notable for its cigar smoke and collection of Elvis decanters, but Lew decided that next time he traveled half way around the world for a bike ride, he would choose a route with even more Wisconsin watering holes.

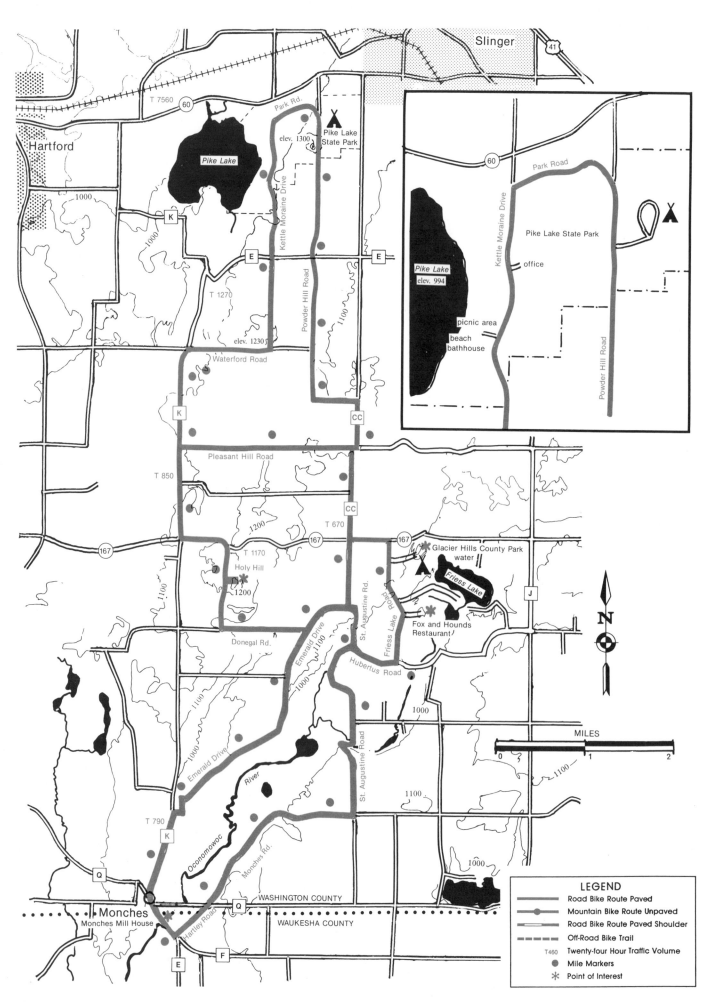

Slinger

Hartford

T 7560

60

Pike Lake

elev. 1300

Park Rd.

Pike Lake State Park

1000

1000

K

E

E

Kettle Moraine Drive

T 1270

Powder Hill Road

1100

elev. 1230

Waterford Road

K

CC

Pleasant Hill Road

T 850

CC

1200

T 670

167

T 1170

167

Glacier Hills County Park
water

Holy Hill

1200

Friess Lake

J

Donegal Rd.

Emerald Drive

1100

St. Augustine Rd.

Friess Lake Road

Fox and Hounds
Restaurant

1000

Hubertus Road

1000

N

Emerald Drive

1100

River

St. Augustine Road

1000

MILES

0   1   2

Oconomowoc

1100

1100

T 790

K

Monches Rd.

1000

Q

WASHINGTON COUNTY

Monches

Q

WAUKESHA COUNTY

Monches Mill House

Hartley Road

E

F

LEGEND

Road Bike Route Paved

Mountain Bike Route Unpaved

Road Bike Route Paved Shoulder

Off-Road Bike Trail

T460   Twenty-four Hour Traffic Volume

Mile Markers

Point of Interest

Pike Lake
elev. 994

60

Park Road

Kettle Moraine Drive

Pike Lake State Park

office

picnic area

beach
bathhouse

Powder Hill Road

36

HOLY HILL RIDE

Enchanting—it's the best description of the forests and marshes surrounding Holy Hill. The kettle moraine topography has given its unique character to this area: there are rolling hills, twisting ridges, kettle lakes and bogs, and also a mix of rock, sand and gravel, which did not lend itself well to farming. Fence rows of glacial boulders cleared from the fields represent hours of back-breaking labor. Consequently this area—just a short drive from greater Milwaukee—has been left in a near wild state.

For the bicyclist, the routes here could hardly be better. Scenic, lightly-traveled roads are abundant, as is wildlife. Once when I was riding along Emerald Drive I spotted what I thought was a small herd of Brown Swiss cows in a field about a quarter-mile away. Slowing my bike and focusing in on the grazing animals, I suddenly realized that they were not cows at all, but bold white-tailed deer abroad in the middle of the day. Stopping by the road, I decided to test their legendary sense of hearing. I released a brake lever, creating the familiar metallic click every bicyclist knows. A second or two later, the time it took for the sound to travel across the field, two heads popped up out of the bunch and looked directly at me.

The area has held great attraction to more than bicyclists and wildlife. The profusion of Irish names on the local roads indicate that the beauty of this land is similar to that of the Emerald Isle. One of my favorite stories recalls an Irish pioneer who was asked why he chose to live near Holy Hill rather than on the more easily farmed lowlands. The Irishman snapped, "We didn't come halfway across a continent to be bog trotters."

At Rudy and Onny's tavern, the only tap in Monches, bicyclists will find both beer and ice cream. This is a particularly popular place during the annual Tour of Holy Hill bicycle race, held on the loop made by Emerald Drive, St. Augustine, and Monches roads. If you can plan ahead, another spot worth considering is the Mill House Tea Room on the shore of the mill pond at the edge of town. You can lunch in this beautiful, early American setting on Wednesdays and Fridays by appointment only from May 15 through December. The owners of this wonderful 1842 stone house also offer bed-and-breakfast rooms. For information contact Harvey and Elaine Taylor at 414-966-7546.

The silhouette of the twin spires of Holy Hill is a frequent landmark along many of the roads on this ride. I won't tell you where to look—I would rather have you be surprised by the beauty of the copper-sheathed steeples piercing the sky. If you would like a closer look you can take on the challenge of the hill that this Carmelite monastery sits on. The religious significance of the spot stems from the miraculous cure experienced by a French hermit at this site in the middle of the last century. The hermit worshipped at a crude cross and today hundreds of thousands visit the shrine.

If you are interested in camping or swimming you might consider Pike Lake State Park; its clear waters were also favored by Indians in prehistoric times. Another fine park is Glacier Hills, a Washington County park on the shores of Friess Lake. You can tent camp there or rent a small cabin. For information call 414-628-1060. Mountain bikers will enjoy the park's wide cross-country trail system. The name Glacier Hills should tip you off that there is some challenge to be had here. The park also includes a lovely bog choked with tamarack trees, which you usually have to travel to northern Wisconsin to enjoy.

You will find the Fox and Hounds Restaurant nearby, one of the state's outstanding eating places, which you will be happy to know serves a luncheon menu from 11:30 a.m. to 3 p.m. Tuesday through Saturday, in addition to Sunday brunch. The core structure of the restaurant is an 1845 vintage log cabin. The beauty of the rustic structure is matched by a lush wilderness setting, which makes this a wonderful place to relax and refuel after a day's ride.

The striking silhouette of Holy Hill.

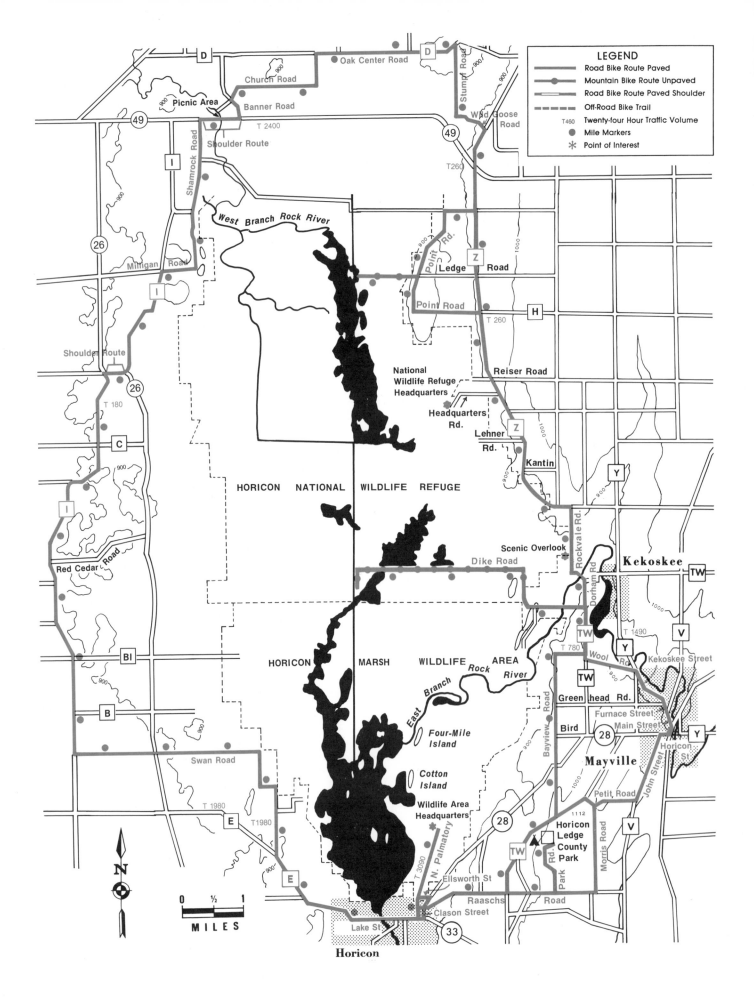

LEGEND
Road Bike Route Paved
Mountain Bike Route Unpaved
Road Bike Route Paved Shoulder
Off-Road Bike Trail
T460 Twenty-four Hour Traffic Volume
Mile Markers
* Point of Interest

D
Oak Center Road
D
Church Road
Stumpf Road
Wild Goose Road
Picnic Area
49
Banner Road
T 2400
49
Shoulder Route
I
T 260
Shamrock Road
West Branch Rock River
26
Point Rd.
Z Road
Milligan Road
Ledge
I
Point Road
H
T 260
Shoulder Route
Reiser Road
26
T 180
National Wildlife Refuge Headquarters
Z
Headquarters Rd.
Lehner Rd.
C
Kantin
Z
Y
I
Scenic Overlook
Kekoskee
Red Cedar Road
Dike Road
TW
Rockvale Rd.
Dorham Rd.
HORICON NATIONAL WILDLIFE REFUGE
1000
TW
T 1490
V
HORICON MARSH WILDLIFE AREA
Rock River
Y
TW
Wool Rd.
Kekoskee Street
BI
East Branch
Bayview Road
Green head Rd.
Furnace Street
B
Four-Mile Island
Bird
28
Main Street
Y
Mayville
Horicon St.
Swan Road
Cotton Island
Petit Road
T 1980
Wildlife Area Headquarters
28
1112
V
E
T 1980
Horicon Ledge County Park
Morris Road
TW
Park Rd.
N. Palmatory
John Street
E
Ellsworth St
Raaschs Road
Lake St
Clason Street
33
Horicon

N

0   ½   1
MILES

HORICON MARSH RIDE

A marsh is a geographical feature I often associate with the character of Wisconsin. Because of its inherent inhospitality to man, marshes are havens for a variety of shy wild creatures. A surface that can't support a man or machine supports vast numbers of migrating waterfowl and provides food, nesting and resting places.

Horicon is the largest of the many marshes that dot Wisconsin. Over 200 species of birds have been sighted here, and the number of migrating geese visiting the Horicon area ranges as high as 70,000. An average of over 5,000 ducks are born here annually. A bicycle and a pair of binoculars are your tickets to an unobtrusive encounter with Horicon's fascinating wild life.

Horicon Marsh owes its existence, as do most Wisconsin marshlands, to the glacier's reshaping of the land. The basin cradling the marsh was carved by the Green Bay lobe during the last glacial epoch about 10,000 years ago. If you look at a map of the state, you can trace the southwestern push of this lobe. The tough Niagara limestone that underlies the Door County peninsula, forming Green Bay, Lake Winnebago and Horicon Marsh, split this lobe off from the Lake Michigan lobe. The ledge rising to form the marsh's eastern boundary, and providing a grand overview of it, is also composed of Niagara limestone. You can camp on top in a gorgeous stand of maple trees at Horicon Ledge County Park.

A variety of excursions are possible in this area, including a 50-mile loop that will take you all the way around the marsh. Although you seldom glimpse the marsh while pedaling through the low farmland along the west side, this is actually the best area to see the gray and black Canada goose. Leftover corn in the fields attracts them in such numbers that at first you may wonder what strange dark crop is blanketing the land. If you take this long loop, remember that Mayville and Horicon, both blessed with fine bakeries and restaurants, are the on-

ly places along the route where you will find food or drink.

The heart of the marsh can be penetrated in three places. In each location the gravel surface makes a fat-tired bike your best choice. The confidence these machines give you on the loose surface allows you to keep your head up—you'll have a better chance of spotting birds. On Ledge Road, a marsh hawk I scared up came so close, I felt the swoosh of its wings. With patience and binoculars you might be able to spot some of the herons from Palmatory Road. These birds have a rookery on Four Mile Island.

Dike Road will take you deepest into the marsh and may offer an opportunity to observe Horicon's most prodigious resident mammal, the muskrat. These industrious, often oblivious critters serve an important purpose in maintaining the delicate balance of the marsh environment. They eat all the cattails they can.

The dike that the road runs on is used today to help regulate water level. It also serves as a reminder of unfortunate at-

tempts to change the marsh. In 1846, a mill built at Horicon turned this one-time Winnebago Indian hunting ground into the largest artificial lake in the world. Twenty years of lawsuits by pioneer farmers, whose lands had been flooded, finally resulted in the removal of the dam and the area's reversion to marshland.

The respite was short-lived, however, as the land hunger at the turn of the century brought extensive ditching and diking attempts designed to make the marsh suitable for agriculture. These efforts failed, and in the '20s, a rising conservation movement eventually brought about the creation of the National Wildlife Refuge in 1941. In 1942, only an estimated 450 geese passed through the marsh. The numbers today are a great testimony to the benefits of the conservation movement.

Stop at either the state or national headquarters for information on what kinds of wildlife may be seen in the marsh during your visit.

In spring and fall, Horicon Marsh is a resting place for some 70,000 migrating geese.

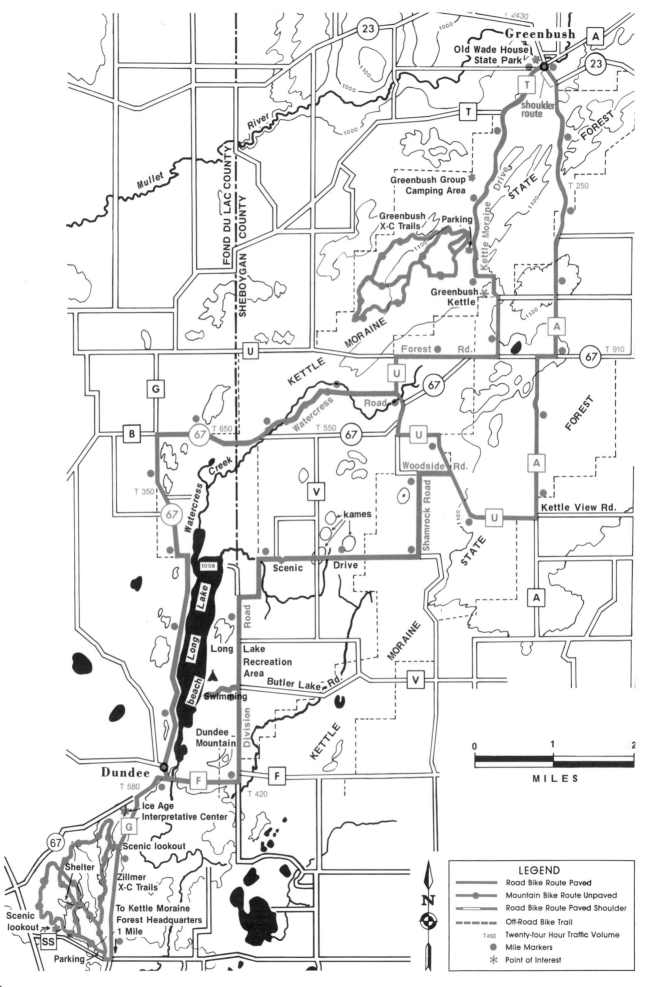

Greenbush

23
A
Old Wade House State Park
shoulder route
T
23
T 2430
1000
1100
1000

Mullet

River

FOND DU LAC COUNTY
SHEBOYGAN COUNTY

Greenbush Group Camping Area

Greenbush X-C Trails Parking

Kettle Moraine Drive

STATE

FOREST

1100
T 250
1100

T

Greenbush Kettle

1100

MORAINE

Forest   Rd.

A

U

KETTLE

Watercress   Road

67

U

67
T 910

U

FOREST

G

B

67 T 650

Watercress T 550 **67**

Creek

Woodside   Rd.

U

A

T 350

67

V

kames

Shamrock Road

U

Kettle View Rd.

1100

Scenic   Drive

STATE

1008

Long   Lake

Road

A

Long Lake Recreation Area

MORAINE

Butler Lake Rd.

V

beach

Swimming

Division

KETTLE

Dundee Mountain

Dundee
T 580
F
F
T 420

Ice Age Interpretative Center

G

67

Scenic lookout

Shelter

Zillmer X-C Trails

To Kettle Moraine Forest Headquarters 1 Mile

Scenic lookout

SS

Parking

0   1   2
MILES

N

LEGEND
Road Bike Route Paved
Mountain Bike Route Unpaved
Road Bike Route Paved Shoulder
Off-Road Bike Trail
T460   Twenty-four Hour Traffic Volume
●   Mile Markers
✳   Point of Interest

NORTHERN KETTLE MORAINE RIDE

Kames, eskers and kettles. They sound like points of interest along some elfin tour. Indeed, it is easy enough to suspect supernatural forces as you cycle through the other-worldly terrain of the kettle moraine. Each bend of the road reveals strange wonders, caldronlike pits, ridges like hibernating serpents and cupcake-shaped hills popping up in unlikely places. You can understand why the Irish considered such earth forms the habitat of wee folk. Like elfin magic, the glacier performed its monumental works when no one was around and left few clues. If it hadn't been for the study of alpine glaciers in the 1800s, we might never have caught on.

The northern kettle moraine offers excellent on-road and off-road bicycling opportunities. On the pavement, you can cruise up and down the spine of the moraine. Like Long Lake, things tend to be linear here due to the glacial ice. The hardwood forest that covers the land doesn't mean people didn't try to homestead the area; the earth simply resisted their attempts. At the intersection of Scenic Drive and County V you can examine a cross-section of a partially excavated kame. It's clear that this land wouldn't be easy to run a plow through. Kames resulted from waterfalls within the ice mass that deposited rocks and dirt in neat, cone-shaped piles.

Stop for a look at the Greenbush Kettle as you ride Kettle Moraine Drive. You will see a huge water-filled pit with a placid surface that mirrors the oaks and maples surrounding it. It formed when a gigantic buried block of ice eventually melted.

The Zillmer and Greenbush cross-country ski trail systems are great places to put a mountain bike through its paces. Both have wide-mowed grass or forest floor trails, well-marked with the appropriate trail color painted on trees or posts. The cobbled nature of the Greenbush trails make them more of a challenge to your riding skill. They lie mainly in deep woods. The Zillmer trails offer a mix of wooded and open landscape.

Glacial kames, kettles, and eskers create a surprising, rolling route through the Northern Kettle Moraine.

Heading north on the yellow trail of the Zillmer system, you can climb and ride along the crest of an esker, a narrow sinuous ridge of debris collected in the bed of a river that flowed through the ice mass. From its lofty height, you will have a gorgeous view of a parallel ridge of moraine and the Dundee Mountain Kame off to the northeast. I recommend using these trails at times other than fall color weekends when hikers flock in.

If you're interested in camping, Long Lake offers 200 sites as well as a fine sandy swimming beach. Firewood is available. If you would rather have someone else do the cooking, I can recommend the food and the prices at the Kettleaire Restaurant "in the loop" in Dundee.

A visit to Old Wade House, a 19th century stagecoach inn, will show you the comforts to be had before people traveled by bicycle. Highway 23, originally a plank road, the "I" road of its day,

seemed a perfect stagestop to the enterprising Yankee, Sylvanus Wade. He built the shining white wilderness oasis in the Greek Revival style, with its classic low-pitched roof, pediment, colonnade and perfect proportions. Before the Civil War, many such homes were built in Wisconsin from pattern books carried west by carpenters with no formal architectural training.

Today, the State Historical Society maintains Old Wade House and brings the past to life with demonstrations of bygone skills, crafts and celebrations, such as Grant's victory at Vicksburg. You can tour this living museum from May through October and for a slight additional fee, enjoy a horse-drawn carriage ride. Included in the tour is a visit to the Jung Carriage Museum where nearly a hundred examples of the wainwright's skill, from fire wagons to elegant coaches, are displayed.

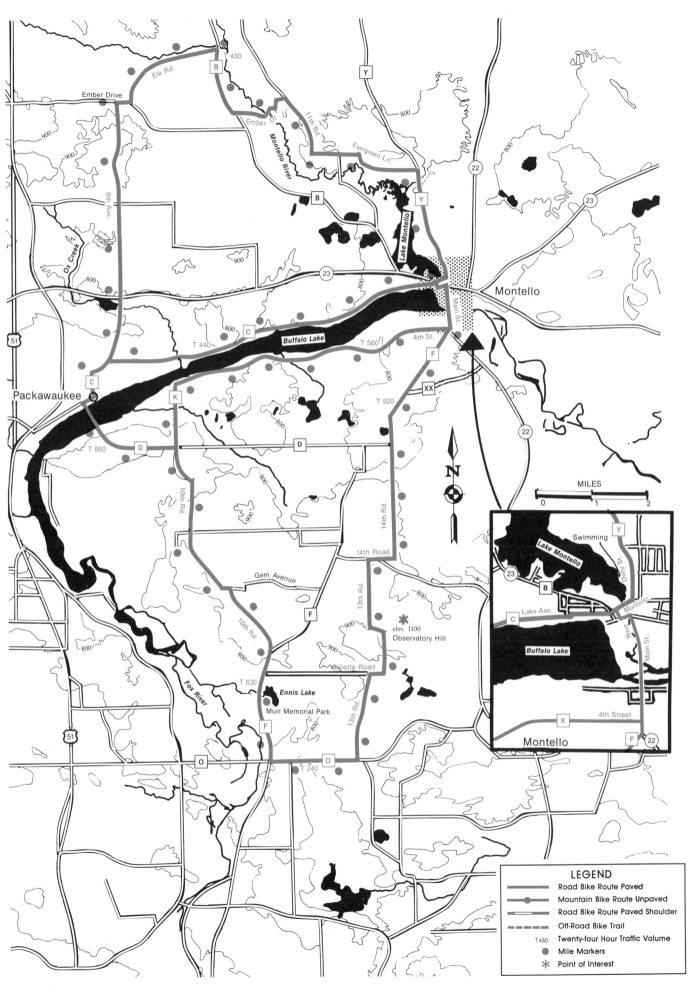

LEGEND

———	Road Bike Route Paved
——•——	Mountain Bike Route Unpaved
——⊥——	Road Bike Route Paved Shoulder
- - - -	Off-Road Bike Trail
T460	Twenty-four Hour Traffic Volume
●	Mile Markers
✱	Point of Interest

42

MONTELLO RIDE

The focus of this ride through gently rolling Marquette County is on a Scottish boy who grew to manhood on the Wisconsin frontier. His name was John Muir. The twenty-five mile route shouldn't be a strain on anyone, though there is a shorter seventeen-mile route and a longer thirty-three-mile route. Any type of bicycle will do for this ride.

Muir Memorial Park, site of the family's first homestead, is on the shore of Ennis Lake on County F. The Muirs' emigration to the new world in 1849 was a sudden change for eleven-year-old John, but along the quiet lakeshore he discovered "that glorious Wisconsin wilderness . . . Here without knowing it we were still at school; every wild lesson a love lesson, not whipped but charmed into us."

From the day they first discovered a blue jay's nest, John and his brother David felt they were in a paradise of birds. Thrushes, meadowlarks, robins, and vociferous redwing blackbirds still flit among the oak groves and across the undulating prairie. Chevrons of geese pattern the sky during the annual spring and fall migrations. At the end of an October day, as I rolled along the causeway across Buffalo Lake south of Packwaukee, thousands of slate-gray coots caught my eye. In the setting sun they were almost indistinguishable from the flashing wavelets.

The coots flourish because of Muir-inspired conservation practices, but such measures came too late to save the creature he considered most wonderful of all, the passenger pigeon. "I have seen flocks streaming south in the fall so large that they were flowing over from horizon to horizon in an almost continuous stream all day long . . . like a mighty river in the sky . . . 'Oh, what bonnie, bonnie birds!' we exclaimed over the first that fell into our hands. 'Oh, what colors! Look at their breasts, bonnie as roses, and at their necks aglow wi' every color . . . Where did they a'come fra, and where are they a' gan? It's awfu' like a sin to kill them!' "

All that is left now is Muir's eloquence, an empty sky, and a lesson.

Montello is a pleasant little town built around an abandoned quarry where famous Montello Red granite was quarried. The comfortable restaurants and stores along the tidy streets and the city swimming beach may tempt you to stay longer. North of town the route parallels the Montello River, through flat, brushy bottomland forest and over a wood-planked, one-lane iron bridge.

Along 13th Road south of Montello, your route skirts Observatory Hill, the highest point in the county. Seventy years ago a hiker found the letters "J. Muir" carved into a tree at the top of the hill. The Muir boys scrambled up the trackless slopes on their infrequent days off. Their stern father allowed only two holidays each year, January 1 and July 4. Such toil appears to have been common, as Muir noted, "Many of our old neighbors . . . grubbed themselves into their graves . . . vaguely trying to get rich, while bread and raiment might have been serenely won on less than a fourth of [their] land . . . ."

By 1867 Muir was on his way to becoming a successful inventor when an accident in an Indiana factory temporarily blinded one eye. During the month he spent in the hospital he came to realize how important his relationship with nature was to him. This insight changed his life and ours. Upon recovering, Muir set off for the wilderness, not to tame it with machines, but to preserve it for all.

His life's work resulted in the creation of the national park system, and he left with us the reassurance that time spent in nature's soothing company is never wasted.

This route winds around pleasant countryside and Montello, where you'll find a swimming beach and many good restaurants.

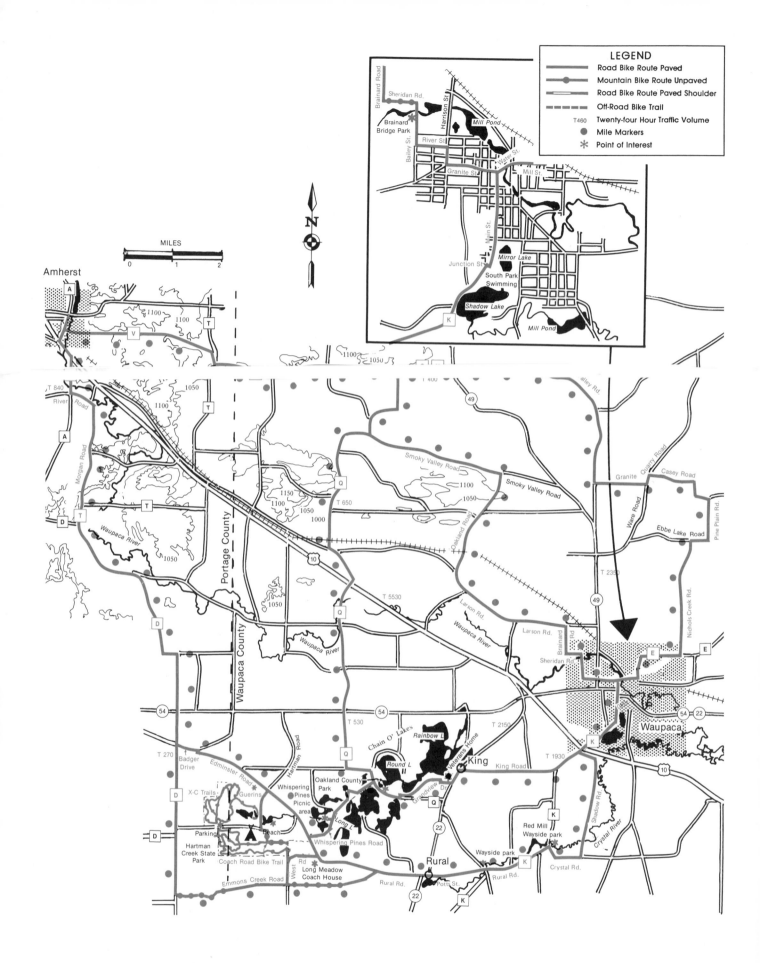

LEGEND

Road Bike Route Paved
Mountain Bike Route Unpaved
Road Bike Route Paved Shoulder
Off-Road Bike Trail
T460	Twenty-four Hour Traffic Volume
●	Mile Markers
✳	Point of Interest

MILES
0   1   2

N

Amherst

Brainard Road
Sheridan Rd.
Brainard Bridge Park
Harrison St.
Mill Pond
Bailey St.
River St.
Granite St.
Mill St.
Main St.
Junction St.
Mirror Lake
South Park Swimming
Shadow Lake
Water St.
Mill Pond
K

1100   1100
V   T
1100   1050

River Road   T 840
Morgan Road   1050
1100
T   T
A
D   T   T
Waupaca River
1050
1050
D
Portage County
Waupaca County
1150
1100
1000
1050
T 650
Q
Waupaca River
1050
10
Q
T 5530
Oakland Road
Larson Rd.
Waupaca River
Larson Rd.
T 400
49
Smoky Valley Road
1100
1050
Smoky Valley Road
Granite   Casey Road
Quarry Trail
Ware Road
Ebbe Lake Road
Pine Plain Rd.
Nichols Creek Rd.
T 2350
49
Brainard Rd.
Sheridan Rd.
E   E
K
54   22
Waupaca

54
D
54
T 530
Q
Chain O' Lakes
Rainbow L
Round L
Veterans Home
King
King Road
T 2150
T 1930
10
T 270   Badger Drive
Edminster Road
Hartman Road
X-C Trails
Guerins
Whispering Pines Picnic area
Oakland County Park
Grandview Dr.
Q
22
Shadow Rd.
Red Mill Wayside park
K
Crystal River
D
Parking
Beach
Long L
Hartman Creek State Park
Coach Road Bike Trail
Whispering Pines Road
Wayside park
K
Crystal Rd.
Emmons Creek Road
West Rd
Long Meadow Coach House
Rural Rd.
Rural
Rural Rd.
Potts St.
22
K

44

WAUPACA RIDE

Vacationland is a term often applied to the Waupaca area. To many, the word conjures up images of fishing and boating, but the area's sometimes forgotten trails and back roads offer scenic adventure to both off-and-on-road bicyclists. The rocky, rolling terrain left behind by the Wisconsin glacial epoch didn't lend itself to agriculture, though it was offered to settlers for pennies an acre. Few farms survive today. Second growth forest harbors abundant wildlife, including a large population of white-tailed deer, which are most likely seen either early or late in the day.

For an enjoyable, short, on-pavement ride, head south from Waupaca on Shadow Road. A turn west on Crystal Road will take you to a pleasant rest stop at the junction of County K, site of the picturesque Red Mill, now an antique shop. You can also view this pioneer building, with its huge water wheel, from an equally beautiful little park just below in a bend of the Crystal River. Continue west through Rural and then back on Whispering Pines and Grandview roads. Several wayside parks offer a chance to stop and rest.

If you like long distances, your reward will be some of the prettiest roads I've ever ridden. During my last visit, the fall color along Smoky Valley Road blended every imaginable bright hue, and Oakland Road tunneled through the vivid yellow canopy of a grove of maples. Overviews of the Little Wolf and Waupaca rivers accent the ride along Morgan and Elm Valley roads. Afterwards, you may find carboloading necessary. If so, I challenge you to try to eat more than five dollars worth of food at the Waupaca Cafe and still get back on your bike.

Hartman Creek State Park offers relaxing camping on the shore of tree-sheltered Allen Lake. Swimming in nearby Hartman Lake is equally appealing, and you can find refreshment at Guerins, near the park entrance. Just look for the sign that advertises "pizza and food." For the mountain biker, Hartman Creek and

For a refreshing break during a day's ride, stop at one of the Waupaca Chain O'Lakes.

the surrounding roads present a variety of experiences. There's some fine riding on the well-marked and wide Oak Ridge cross-country ski trail system that laces the west end of the park. You'll find the most scenic and enjoyable riding on the trails rated "more" and "most" difficult. In spite of the rating, they are really not very difficult. The trails rated easy tend to be located in tree plantations where the surface is soft and sandy.

A bike trail in Hartman Creek Park makes an enjoyable, easy mountain bike ride. It follows a portion of the old stage coach route from Oshkosh to Stevens Point. Its grassy surface is just fine for fat tires. At the edge of the park, the trail junctions with West Road. If you follow West Road to the east, it will take you to Rural Road and Long Meadow Coach House, an old stage coach inn

that is now a beautifully maintained private residence. Rural and Emmons roads have been designated Rustic Roads to preserve their character and protect them from development. They lead you on a scenic, fat-tired tour around the park.

Over the past dozen years the state Rustic Roads board and the Department of Transportation have identified over 30 unique roads in Wisconsin worthy of preservation. The rustic roads movement recognizes that a road can be more than a utilitarian passageway: the aesthetics of the roadside, the curve of the road and the way it lies upon the land make travel more than transporation—as every bicyclist already knows.

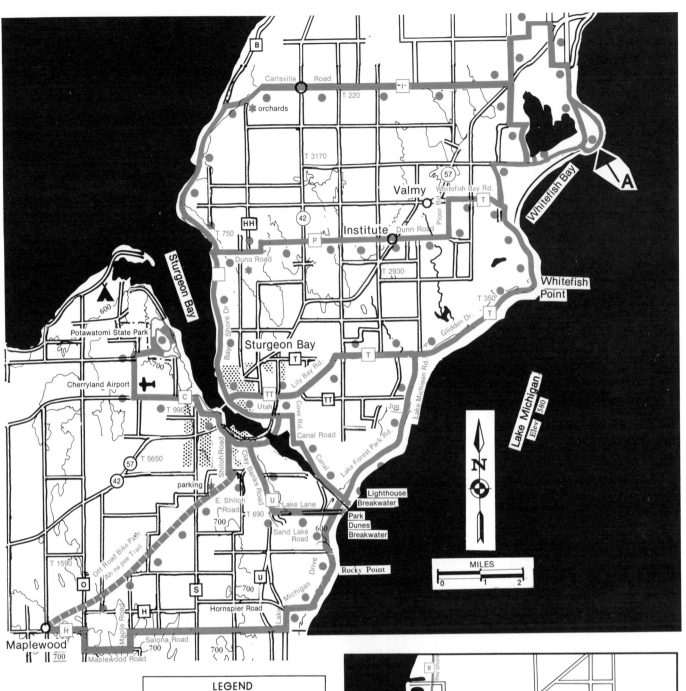

B

Carlsville Road
T 220

orchards

T 3170

57
Valmy
42
Whitefish Bay Rd.
Institute
HH
P
Dunn Road
T 750
Ploor Rd.
T
A
Whitefish Bay

Dunn Road
T 2930
Whitefish
Point

Sturgeon Bay

600
T 350
T

Potawatomi State Park
700
Glidden Dr.
T

Sturgeon Bay
Bay Shore Dr
T
Lily Bay Rd.

Cherryland Airport
C
Lake Michigan Rd.
Lake Michigan
Elev 580

T 990
Utah
TT
Cove Rd.
TT
Jog

Shiloh Road
Canal Road

57
T 5650
Clay Banks Road
Canal

42
parking
U
Lake Lane
Lighthouse
Breakwater

N

E. Shiloh Road
T 690
Park
Dunes
Breakwater

Sand Lake Road
600
Off Road Bike Path
Ah na pee Trail
Rocky Point

T 1590
O
700
Lake Michigan Drive
700

S
700
MILES

H
Hornspier Road
U

Maplewood
H
Salona Road
700
700

Maple Road
Maplewood Road
700

0   1   2

LEGEND
Road Bike Route Paved
Mountain Bike Route Unpaved
Road Bike Route Paved Shoulder
Off-Road Bike Trail
T460   Twenty-four Hour Traffic Volume
Mile Markers
* Point of Interest

B
Bay Shore

Bus. 57
42

Maritime Museum

N. 3rd Ave.

Bay Ship Yard

Iowa
Door Cty.
Historical Museum
Michigan St.
W. Elm Ave.

C
TT

W. Hickory

Palmer
Johnson Co.
swimming
Pennsylvania
Memorial Dr.
Utah

N. 1st Ave.
E. Maple

Madison St
W. Maple St.
Peterson Builders

Bayview
Bridge

S. Neenah Ave.
S. Oxford Ave.

Circle Ridge
Road
Cove Rd.

E. Walnut
42
57
Clay Banks Rd.

Tacoma   Beach Rd.

Shiloh Road
U

Sturgeon Bay

STURGEON BAY/CAVE POINT RIDE

The Great Lakes are America's inland sea. If this has never made much of an impression on you, a visit to Sturgeon Bay and Cave Point will change your mind forever. Sturgeon Bay is the largest ship-building port on the lakes. This is a no-nonsense, heavy industry. At Cave Point every crashing wave will give you a sense of the power of Lake Michigan.

Ever-present sea gulls also remind you of the maritime focus of the area. Even far inland, you will see them soaring. To explore the interior of the peninsula south of Sturgeon Bay, I recommend riding a fat-tired or mountain bike. The Ahnapee State Trail has fallen into a state uncomfortable for a skinny-tired bicycle rider. With fat tires, however, I think you will find the little park at the north end of Lake Michigan Drive a terrific spot to wiggle your toes in the sand and watch the ships and sailboats gliding past the canal lighthouse.

If your destination is the other side of the channel, you can avoid riding through Sturgeon Bay by taking the bike path over the new Bayview Bridge. I should emphasize the word "path" here, because it is little more than that. It is well-marked—you would never find it among the weeds otherwise—and the view from the bridge is terrific. Still, bypassing the town may be a mistake. Breakfast at the Fisherman's Table, near the south end of the old bridge, was such a great deal I recommend it highly.

Cross the old bridge on the wooden sidewalk; it's not as unsettling as the open grate of the roadway. The drawbridge goes up on the hour to let sailboats pass through. At the north end, a dock lined with sleek-looking sailboats will catch your eye. This is the Palmer Johnson works where luxury yachts are crafted for discriminating—and rich—sailors from all over the world. At First Avenue you can turn right or left for a look at more work-a-day vessels taking shape. To the right is Peterson Builders. If it's a hot day and their doors are open, you can watch them build everything from wooden minesweepers to steel tuna boats.

To the left of Palmer Johnson is Bay Ship, which builds gigantic, thousand-foot freighters. The little park on the north side of the shipyard is a good place to watch the activity. There is also the Maritime Museum lodged in the pilot house of an old freighter. If you like food with your ships, try dinner at the Nautical Inn on Michigan Street. Great meals are served by nice folks.

Potawatomi State Park, a fine place to camp, features a special area for bicycle campers. If you are travelling by car you will need campsite reservations in advance, even during midweek. The same is true if you intend to stay at a motel.

North of Sturgeon Bay, you can choose between three on-road loops. The longest will take you to Cave Point. As you pedal north on County B, you may find the orchard-covered hills rising to the east another attraction. At Carlsville you can sample the fruit, and for a fee, you can tour the Door Peninsula Winery, in an old schoolhouse, where Door County cherry, apple, and pear wines are served with Wisconsin cheese.

You'll know you're near Cave Point when you hear thunder, and the sky is cloudless. Walk to the edge of the rocky, 30-foot high bluffs and look down. Below, waves roll into the huge caves that give the point its name. You can actually feel the rock tremble beneath your feet as the waves crash. Towards the end of the last century, a night storm drove a schooner upon these rocks. Only one man lived through it. He awoke next morning in a cleft high in the rock with no idea of how he had survived.

Just south of Cave Point, the lake has a different character. The crescent beach of Whitefish Bay and the dunes behind it are themselves wavelike. The quiet harmony of wave and shore contrasts sharply with the pounding just a mile to the north. Spend a day at Whitefish Dunes State Park relaxing on the beach.

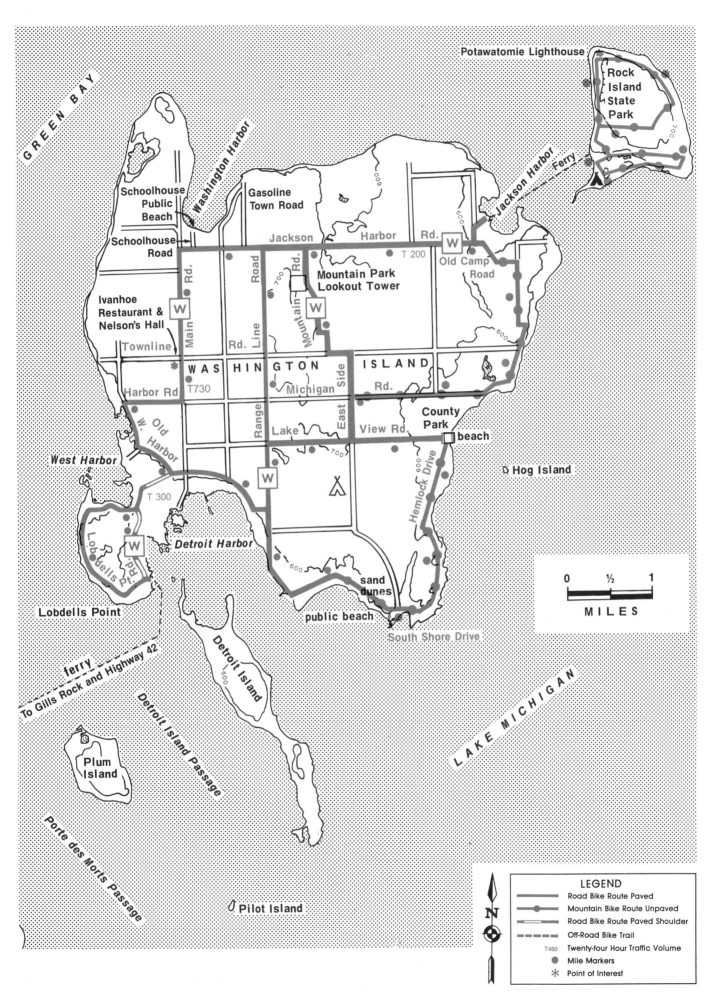

GREEN BAY

Potawatomie Lighthouse

Rock
Island
State
Park

Jackson Harbor   Ferry

Schoolhouse
Public
Beach

Washington Harbor

Gasoline
Town Road

Schoolhouse
Road

Jackson   Harbor   Rd.

T 200

Old Camp
Road

Mountain Park
Lookout Tower

Ivanhoe
Restaurant &
Nelson's Hall

Townline

Main   Rd.

Road   Line

Rd.   Line

Mountain   Rd.

WASHINGTON   ISLAND

East Side

Harbor Rd.   T730

Michigan   Rd.

Range

Lake   View Rd.

County
Park

beach

West Harbor

Old   W. Harbor

T 300

Hog Island

Hemlock Drive

Lobdells Pt.   Rd.

Detroit Harbor

sand
dunes

public beach

South Shore Drive

Lobdells Point

ferry
To Gills Rock and Highway 42

Detroit Island Passage

Detroit Island

LAKE MICHIGAN

Plum
Island

Porte des Morts Passage

Pilot Island

0   ½   1

MILES

N

LEGEND

Road Bike Route Paved
Mountain Bike Route Unpaved
Road Bike Route Paved Shoulder
Off-Road Bike Trail
T460   Twenty-four Hour Traffic Volume
Mile Markers
Point of Interest

WASHINGTON ISLAND/ ROCK ISLAND RIDE

When the midsummer heat softens the pavement, it's time to head for Washington and Rock islands. The breezes wafting off Green Bay and Lake Michigan keep the islands cool while the rest of the Midwest swelters. This means you may occasionally need a sweater or windbreaker.

Bicyclists have discerned the islands' perfect temperatures. Harbor Bike Rental at Lobdells Point has a fleet of 90, and on a summer day there were only a half-dozen left unrented. Not that I minded; the heightened interest in bicycling is responsible for the addition of a paved shoulder along County W between the ferry dock and Old West Harbor Road.

You will need to schedule your tour carefully, especially if your visit is in the spring or fall or if you intend to spend time on Rock Island. Your adventure begins wtih the ferry ride, and this part of the trip emphasizes the mystery and isolation of the island people, who have chosen to live in the past and have an investment in that isolation. There always seems to be enough room for another bicycle on the Washington Island ferry; the cruise—about $3.25 one way with bicycle—takes the better part of an hour and the schedule is abbreviated before the Fourth of July and after Labor Day. *Karfi*, the Rock Island ferry, runs from 10 a.m. to 4 p.m. and charges about $3.50 per round trip plus an additional $2 for your bike.

The appeal of the islands today seems to be their slower pace. In the past, they beckoned as a refuge, a stepping stone on the path of exploration or a New World home for people from another isolated island.

Indians have lived here since the early years of the Christian era. In the mid-1600s, they sheltered the Potawatomi fleeing the rigors of the Iroquois War. A war party of 800 Iroquois was soon dispatched from New York; the Potawatomi withdrew to a peninsula with a reliable water supply and withstood a siege that lasted two years.

The list of French explorers who stop-ped here reads like a Who's Who of North American discovery: Duluth, Nicolet, La Salle, Marquette and Joliet, to name a few. La Salle, starting the trend, arrived in 1679 on the *Griffin*, the first European-type craft on the Great Lakes. He loaded it with furs bound for Montreal and then set off himself by canoe for the Mississippi. The *Griffin* was never heard from again. Since then, over 50 sailing ships are known to have perished in the treacherous island waters. No wonder the French named the channel *Porte des Morts*, or Death's Door.

In the 19th century, Icelandic settlers, to whom isolation was nothing new, arrived on Washington Island. Their ethnic community, the oldest of its kind in the nation, still flourishes here and their crafts and traditions are revived annually in mid-August during Island Fair weekend.

You will find Washington Island's easy terrain and small size handy to pedal about, but if you race through you'll be missing a great deal. What passes for the only town is a collection of stores and taverns strung out along Main Road just north of West Harbor Road. When I was there, the Ivanhoe Restaurant featured tasty perch fillet burgers. Nelson's Hall Tavern is highly recommended and their shaded bicyle-rider's rest stop alongside

There's always room for one more bicycle on the Washington Island Ferry.

the tavern is a nice touch.

If you like to swim or just need some sand in your shoes, there are three public beaches. The east side County Park beach is the most isolated, Sand Dunes Beach has the wonderful character its name implies and School House Public Beach is sheltered by the bright limestone bluffs of Washington Harbor. With a snorkel and mask you can explore the wreck of the freighter *Louisiana*, lying in three to 60 feet of water on the east side of the harbor. For a fine overview of the north end of Washington Island and Rock Island in the distance, climb the steps of the Mountain Park lookout tower, a pleasant stop on Mountain Road. Mountain bike riders will enjoy exploring the smooth gravel roads on the island's east side.

There is a private campground on Washington Island, but if you have camping in mind, I urge you to try Rock Island. I know that once you've enjoyed the peace of its car-free environment, it will always be your destination.

Rock Island has worked its spell on many people. Chester Thordarson, an electrical genius whose inventions made practical the transmission of electrical power over long distances, had Icelandic roots and chose to buy the whole island in 1910. The beautiful stone boat house where the ferry docks was his great hall, inspired by Icelandic Viking lairs.

The wide-mowed grass snowmobile trails lacing the island make for great mountain biking or hiking. At the northern tip stands the Potawatomi lighthouse, the oldest on the lake. Near it, an old wooden stairway leads you down the sheer bluff face to a stony beach, which looks out on St. Martin Island, Michigan. You may not get that far if you pause to sun yourself on a limestone slab or on the sandy beach near the campground. I recommend bringing plenty of food. Once you're on Rock Island, you may feel that missing the boat back is the best thing that could happen to you.

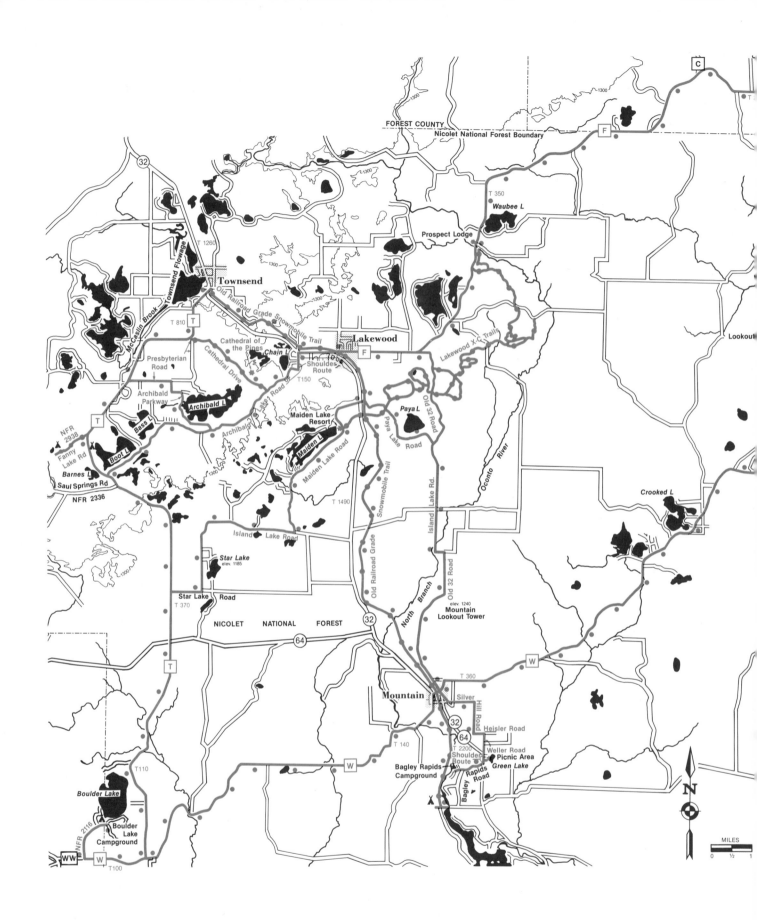

FOREST COUNTY

Nicolet National Forest Boundary

C

F

Waubee L

T 350

Prospect Lodge

Lookout

32

T 1260

Townsend

Old Railroad Grade Snowmobile Trail

Lakewood

Lakewood X-C Trails

F

McCaslin Brook

Townsend Flowage

T 810

T

Cathedral of the Pines

Chain L

Shoulder Route

Presbyterian Road

Cathedral Drive

T 150

Paya L

Old 32 Road

Oconto River

Archibald Parkway

Archibald L

Lake Road

Maiden Lake Resort

Paya Lake Road

NFR 2938

T

Bass

Archibald

Maiden L

Crooked L

Fanny Lake Rd

X

Boot L

Maiden Lake Road

Snowmobile Trail

Island Lake Rd.

Barnes L

Saul Springs Rd

T 1490

NFR 2336

Island Lake Road

Star Lake
elev. 1185

Old Railroad Grade

Old 32 Road

NICOLET NATIONAL FOREST

Star Lake Road

T 370

32

elev. 1240
Mountain Lookout Tower

64

North Branch

W

T

T 360

W

Mountain

Silver

32

Hill Road

Heisler Road

64

T 140

W

T 2200
Shoulder Route

Weller Road

Picnic Area

T 110

Bagley Rapids Campground

Bagley Rapids Road

Green Lake

X

Boulder Lake

N

NFR 2116

Boulder Lake Campground

WW

W

T 100

MILES

0   ½   1

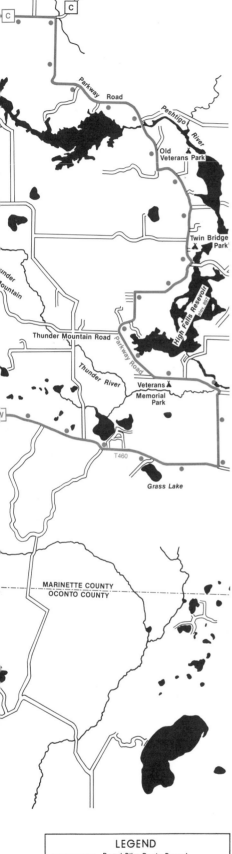

NICOLET NATIONAL FOREST RIDE

When I recently returned to the Mountain area of the Nicolet National Forest, I was pleasantly surprised to see that the roads were being paved up in these parts. Ten years ago, my attempt to lay out a bike route around Mountain, Lakewood, and Townsend, three reduced speed zones on Highway 32, ended in failure. I gave up after my umpteenth encounter with loose gravel.

Beautiful campgrounds can be found throughout the National Forest and at several Marinette County parks along Parkway Road. Their settings are sparkling lake shores or river banks. With such selection, you may want to consider getting to know the forest on a tour of several days.

I don't know how much time Paul Bunyan spent in Lakewood, but he seems to be well thought of by the Holowinskis. They have a huge (but of course it would be) statue of the folktale lumberjack hero in front of their bar. Audrey Holowinski told me about the great cross-country ski trails around Lakewood, which mountain bikers can take all the way from the north end of Maiden Lake to Prospect Lodge on County F. The terrain is never overly severe, but the trail surface makes for slow-going. These are old logging roads, some of which have not been used for many years, judging from the diameter of the tree stumps in the road bed. (They are cut off close to the ground, but it's still tricky riding.) Along the trail you will see even bigger, moss-covered stumps cut off chest-high, decaying remnants of the giant timber stands that once covered this land. A compass is a must; these trails are not mowed and other trails intersect with them. Marking is adequate, consisting of colored ribbons, blue cross-country skier and silhouette signs, and posted maps indicating "you are here."

If you would like to see what the virgin forest was like, take an easy mountain bike ride through the Cathedral of the Pines. The giant trees are about a quarter mile in from Archibald Lake Road. More easy off-road biking is to be had along the old railroad grade/snowmobile trail between Townsend and Mountain. The surface is a bit rough in places, but the scenery is great and there is always an anticipation of Mountain, Lakewood or Townsend, just around the next bend, to keep you going.

Road bikers can enjoy the scenery from road surfaces that vary from excellent to mediocre. As is typical in the Northwoods, pavement is allowed to deteriorate and then resurfacing is done on the worst sections only while the rest is left to decay a few more years. If variety is the spice of life then the Northwoods roads have it all.

No matter what type of bike you are riding through the Nicolet National Forest, your visit cannot be said to be complete without at least one quiet night of Northwoods camping.

LEGEND

▬▬▬	Road Bike Route Paved
▬●▬	Mountain Bike Route Unpaved
▭▭▭	Road Bike Route Paved Shoulder
▬ ▬ ▬	Off-Road Bike Trail
T460	Twenty-four Hour Traffic Volume
●	Mile Markers
✳	Point of Interest

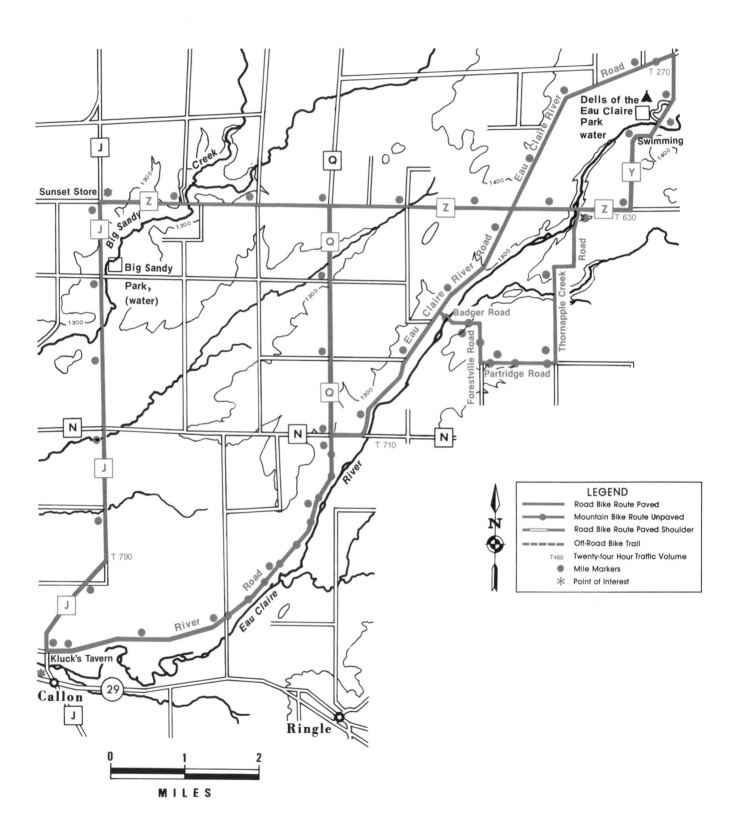

LEGEND

	Road Bike Route Paved
	Mountain Bike Route Unpaved
	Road Bike Route Paved Shoulder
	Off-Road Bike Trail
T460	Twenty-four Hour Traffic Volume
	Mile Markers
*	Point of Interest

0   1   2

MILES

EAU CLAIRE RIVER RIDE

In the center of the state is a county park of rare beauty—the Dells of the Eau Claire. Here you can rest by the cascading falls of the Eau Claire River or swim in calmer waters upstream. The routes cover modest hills and pass farms and woods, so the trip will be pleasant for any rider on any type of bike. Camping is available at Dells of the Eau Claire Park.

Whether you plan to take the twenty-eight-mile or the sixteen-mile route, head north across rolling farmland first, and save the gentle ramble along the river for the home stretch. County Trunk J near the town of Callon is a convenient starting point for the long route, and the junction of county trunks Q and N is a good beginning for the shorter route.

Six miles north of Callon, you come to Big Sandy Park. When I was there in the fall, Big Sandy Creek was dry, but the streambed told an interesting story. The bare stone surface showed layers of ancient rock tilted almost vertically. From the types of rock in outcrops like this one and the pitch of their strata, geologists put together a picture of the surrounding area as it was ages before the earliest forms of life. These tilted rocks, they say, were formed by the intense heat inside huge mountains as tall as the Alps. Nearly a billion years have passed since then, so erosion has had plenty of time to flatten the old mountains into the gentle hills you cover on this tour.

The mountains are certainly well disguised under the modern dairy farms you pass as you ride east on County Trunk Z. To the north on County Trunk Y, more recent geologic forces have left their mark at Dells of the Eau Claire Park. Sixty-foot cliffs were formed here by the boulder-laden meltwater of the last glacier. Part of that glacier's legacy is a waterfall near the park entrance. The Eau Claire River, dyed brown by the tamarack roots at its marshy source, tumbles over a fault and eddies in a deep pool surrounded by walls of smooth rock. When the soft stone under Niagara Falls has eroded away to leave

Eau Claire River at the dells.

a mere rapids, the durable rock here will channel the river much as it does today. Expert swimmers can navigate the dells' swirling waters, but apprentice Tarzans should stick to the more tranquil waters upstream on the east side of County Trunk Y. A hiking trail in the park winds through evergreen forest along the edge of the cliffs for those who want to explore off their bikes.

A short distance north of the park, the tour route turns southwest along the river on Eau Claire River Road. The Eau Claire didn't carve the pretty valley where it

flows toward the Wisconsin—a massive fault caused the bedrock of the river gorge to drop away several hundred million years ago. Eau Claire River Road is seldom within view of the water, but the woods make pleasant scenery, and you can always find a clear path through the gravel stretches. The miles of easy pedaling will be a welcome opportunity to comtemplate the beauty of the Eau Claire dells, and the good feeling of warm air flowing past after a dip in the river will put you in the right mood for thought.

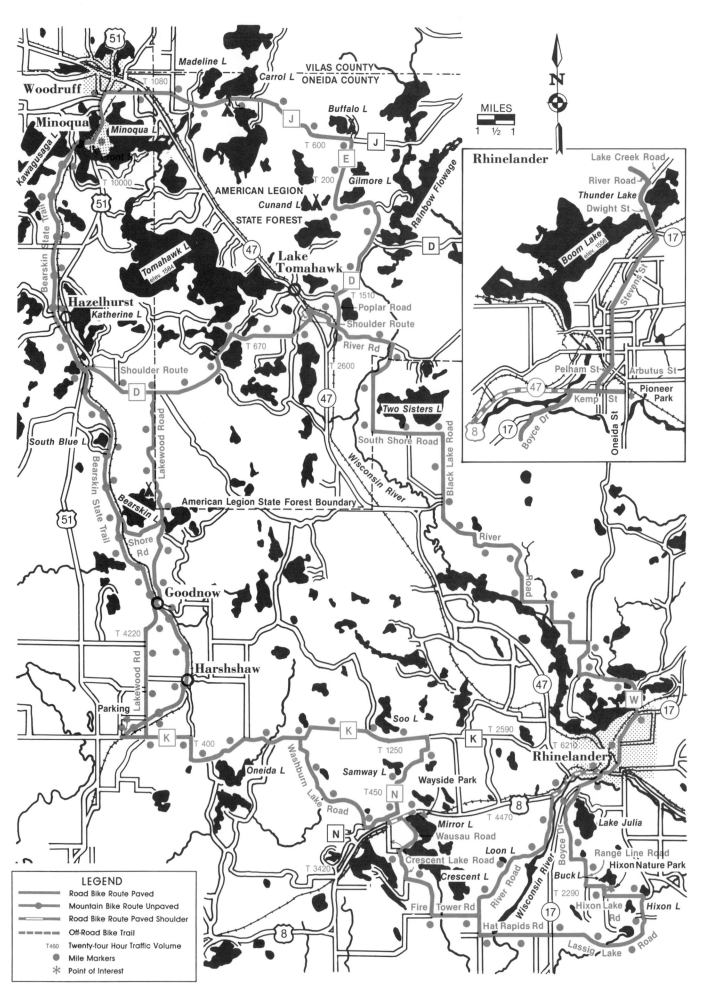

MILES

Rhinelander

LEGEND

	Road Bike Route Paved
	Mountain Bike Route Unpaved
	Road Bike Route Paved Shoulder
	Off-Road Bike Trail
T460	Twenty-four Hour Traffic Volume
●	Mile Markers
✳	Point of Interest

54

RHINELANDER/BEARSKIN TRAIL RIDE

In 1896, a timber cruiser named Gene Shepard came into Rhinelander with the tale of a ferocious beast he had encountered in the woods and a photograph to prove it. Whether Shepard ever intended to actually deceive anyone or simply had a vision of giving the rude lumber town a symbol of civic pride, no one knows. Embellishing his tale with stories of the monster's appetite for white bulldogs, he encouraged the lumberjacks, who had always appreciated a tall tale, to take the creature, called a Hodag, to heart.

To understand how Shepard could pull off a hoax that had newspaper reporters from all over hopping trains to Rhinelander, you need to know a little about timber cruisers. Lumberjacks worked in crews, sledding out the logs during the winter months. The timber cruiser was the scout who set off alone to survey the vast stands of timber during the summer with only the mosquitos and deerflies for company. The timber cruiser was expected to return with a report on the type and quality of trees in an area and the best way to extract them. When he returned, there were two things the timber cruiser could count on: a healthy paycheck and lots of ears eager for news of the vast unknown forest.

Today, your visit to Rhinelander wouldn't be complete without some sort of Hodag encounter. Perhaps you will have a Hodag burger or visit the Hodag Lounge (not shown, but just out of town off Highway 8 east). You can hardly take a photograph without catching the likeness of this toothy monster of the lake and bog; it adorns every lamp post.

In a tall stand of pine in Rhinelander's Pioneer Park, you can visit a reconstructed lumberjack camp: you'll get a glimpse of how these remarkable men lived, and see the saws, axes and tools they used to turn a primeval forest into lumber to build a nation. The Logging Museum, featuring the only genuine replica of a Hodag in captivity, is open daily from mid-May to mid-September and is free, although donations are appreciated.

On your ride through the wild countryside you'll see second growth timber, which is beautiful forest, but scrubby stuff compared to the billion board feet of virgin timber that the lumberjacks originally found here. The fact that these men and their animals, with nothing more than muscle power, made the land as barren as the surface of the moon seems like a tall tale in itself.

Riding south of Rhinelander, you can soak up the beauty of the woods or trace the course of the Wisconsin River and relax at Hixon or Crescent Lake parks, which offer picnicking at pretty lakeside locations. If you are more adventurous, you can range farther north into the Northern Highland-American Legion State Forest, where you'll find campgrounds located in such spectacular settings that you may not want to leave. The backroads are lightly traveled, but if you prefer a completely traffic-free environment, try the Bearskin State Trail. It follows an old railroad grade that will lead you through incomparable Northwoods scenery to the island city of Minocqua, which is almost completely surrounded by water.

Vilas and northern Oneida counties share with parts of Minnesota, Ontario and Finland the distinction of being the most densely lake-covered areas in the world—which means that you will never have any problem finding a quiet stretch of shoreline to enjoy.

If you prefer a completely traffic-free environment, head for the Bearskin State Trail.

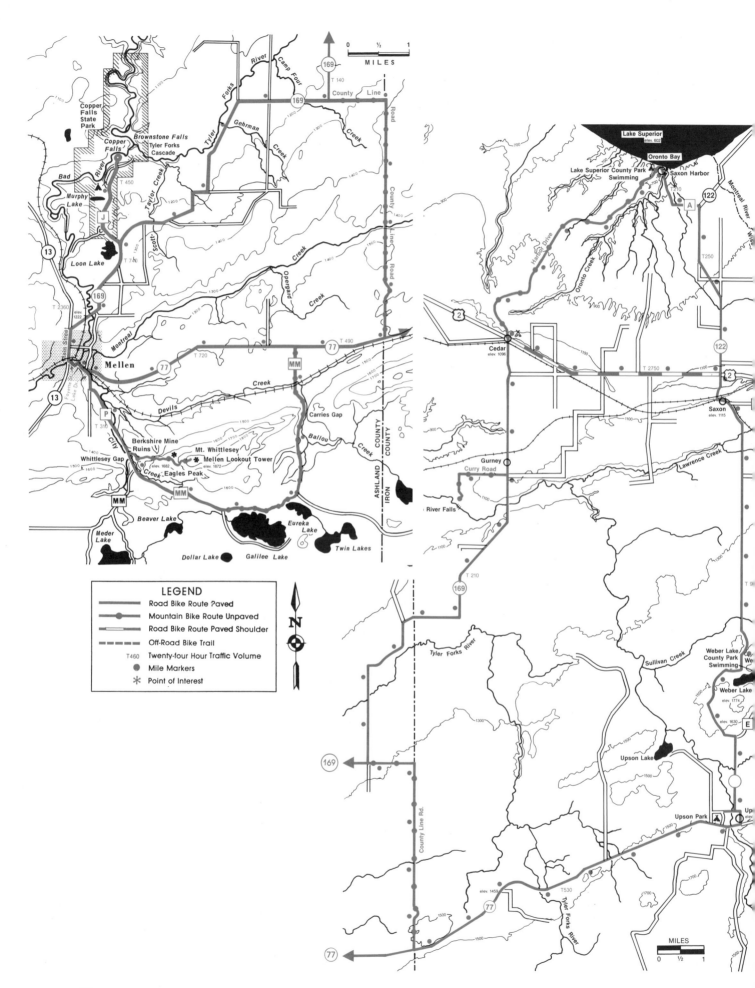

LEGEND
Road Bike Route Paved
Mountain Bike Route Unpaved
Road Bike Route Paved Shoulder
Off-Road Bike Trail
T460   Twenty-four Hour Traffic Volume
●   Mile Markers
✳   Point of Interest

N

COPPER FALLS RIDE

Raw, coarse and compellably beautiful. This is a part of the country where frontiersmen and women spent their lives locked in a struggle with the land itself.

At the turn of the century, lumberjacks cleared and hauled virgin timber to the mills. The tide of immigration brought Finns and Italians to labor in iron mines or homestead the cutover land. Hemingway worked in Mellen for a while before leaving to drive an ambulance for the Italian Army in World War I. Today the land again has the upper hand; abandoned mines and farms dot the resurgent forest.

The 90-mile-long Gogebic Range consists of two parallel rows of hills. Seven hundred million years ago they towered as high as the Alps. Though greatly diminished, the grades that remain have no intention of giving a bicyclist's legs a break. For those with a sense of adventure, there is fine riding. Campsites at Copper Falls State Park, Upson and Saxon Harbor offer the possibility of a two- or three-day tour.

Mountain bike riders can circle Mt. Whittlesey, the highest point in the iron-bearing Gogebic, as they pedal through Whittlesey Gap near Mellen and Carries Gap farther east. On the sandy rocky fire lane winding to the top of Mt. Whittlesey you will find a north-facing rocky overlook. Bring your binoculars—you can see Mellen and Lake Superior beyond. Or, you can outwit the terrain on Highway 77. It isn't dead flat, but it does run relatively level between the two lines of the Gogebics.

As a friend and I prepared for the last ride of the season, on a September day with temperatures in the 40s, I smelled an unmistakable aroma drifting down Mellen's Main Street. Sure enough, Saturday is Cornish pasty day at Nelson's Bakery. After we fortified ourselves with donuts and coffee, we stuffed two hot meat and potato pasties into a fanny pack. We toured Upson and Saxon and, four hours later, stopped at Copper Falls. (Don't expect to find as much as a tavern in Gurney, by the way.) As we watched the brown water of the Bad River cascade over the fractured mass of red lava rock, the traditional miner's fare didn't let us down. The pasties still steamed in the chill air.

You will find a fascinating geologic story at Copper Falls, a story closely linked to the history of Lake Superior itself. The lava in the park did not come from volcanos. It bubbled up through cracks in the earth's crust in a massive flow, 11 miles deep in some places. Under this tremendous weight, the crust subsided and formed the huge basin that now holds the largest body of fresh water in the world, Lake Superior. The numerous falls communicate their own magic through surging water, which is similar but never the same in sound or form as it plunges over rocks.

Besides Copper Falls you can visit Brownstone Falls and Tyler Forks Cascades, also in the park, or take a short side trip near Gurney to Potato River Falls. The latter consists of an upper and lower falls, which tumble through a narrow gorge in a quiet little park.

Your chances of encountering wildlife on your ride is considerably greater than the probability of meeting people. Great birds of prey soar the sky and white-tailed deer are common sights. Once on Mt. Whittlesey, I was toiling through a railroad cut leading to the Berkshire Mine when I startled a large raven that flew over the cut and braked its flight at the sight of me. Because the jagged walls of black ironwood acted as an amplifier, I could hear the deceleration of every feather.

Copper Falls is just one of many spectacular falls you'll see on a hike through the state park.

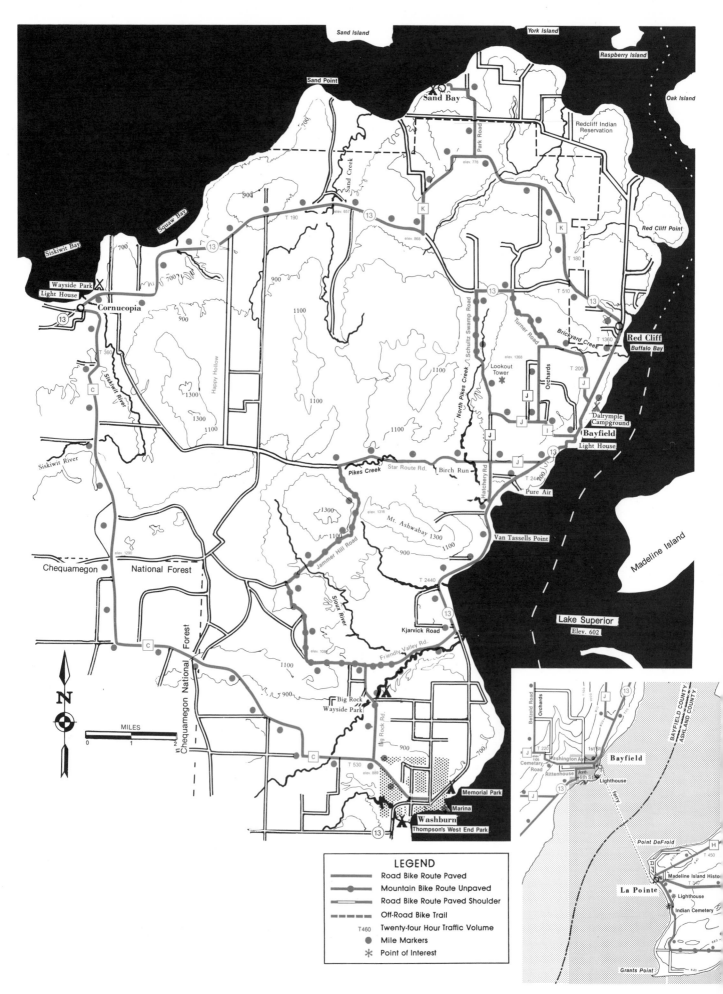

LEGEND
	Road Bike Route Paved
	Mountain Bike Route Unpaved
	Road Bike Route Paved Shoulder
	Off-Road Bike Trail
T460	Twenty-four Hour Traffic Volume
●	Mile Markers
✳	Point of Interest

Sand Island

York Island

Raspberry Island

Oak Island

Sand Point

Sand Bay

Redcliff Indian Reservation

Park Road

elev. 776

Red Cliff Point

Squaw Bay

Sand Creek

elev. 657

K

K

T 180

700

900

T 190

13

13

700

elev. 868

Siskiwit Bay

700

13

T 510

T 1360

13

Wayside Park

Light House

Cornucopia

900

900

Brickyard Creek

Red Cliff

Buffalo Bay

13

T 360

1100

Happy Hollow

1100

North Pikes Creek

Schultz Swamp Road

Turner Road

elev. 1368

Lookout Tower
✳

Orchards

T 200

J

J

Siskiwit River

1300

1300

1100

C

1100

1100

J

J

I

Dalrymple Campground

Bayfield

Light House

Siskiwit River

Pikes Creek

Star Route Rd.

Birch Run

Hatchery Rd.

13

T 244 200

J

Pure Air

1300

elev. 1316

Mt. Ashwabay 1300

900

1100

Van Tassells Point

Chequamegon

National Forest

elev. 1290

Jammer Hill Road

Sioux River

T 2440

Madeline Island

Lake Superior
Elev. 602

C

1100

elev. 100

Kjarvick Road

13

Chequamegon National Forest

Friendly Valley Rd.

N

MILES
0   1   2

1100

900

Big Rock Wayside Park

Big Rock Rd.

C

T 530

elev. 880

900

700

Memorial Park

Marina

13

Washburn

Thompson's West End Park

Betzold Road

Orchards

J

13

BAYFIELD COUNTY
ASHLAND COUNTY

T 220

1st St.

Cemetery Road

Washington Ave.

Rittenhouse

Ave.

4th St.

Bayfield

Lighthouse

J

13

Point DeFroid

T 450

H

Madeline Island Histo

La Pointe

Lighthouse

Indian Cemetery

Grants Point

BAYFIELD/MADELINE ISLAND RIDE

Bayfield remains a picture-postcard fishing village locked in another time. If you think of bicycling not as an end in itself, but as a pleasant way of traveling to and through fascinating places, you'll love visiting this out-of-the-way part of the world with its memorable history, scenery, dining and camping experiences.

Bayfield is a good place to begin and end your ride, no matter how long or hard you want to pedal. You can camp just north of town on Dalrymple City Park, or, if you make reservations early enough, you can find lodging in one of several inns and bed-and-breakfast establishments. The Rittenhouse Inn, an ornate Victorian mansion overlooking the town, has an outstanding reputation for both lodging and dining; reservations are necessary. There are many other restaurants in town, many which specialize in fresh fish because this is where they are caught. Commercial fishing boats bob in the harbor, bringing in their daily haul alongside luxurious sailboats.

The answer to the question of where to go for an easy or hard ride is simple. The easy pedaling is on Madeline Island. Bayfield's hilly streets foreshadow the tough terrain the mainland offers. If you feel like taking on a challenge, the rewards are great. If you have a road bike, consider the loop around Bayfield on County I and J that takes you through the apple orchards. They're snow-white with blossoms in mid-May and heavy with red fruit in late September. Bayfield's Apple Festival celebrates the harvest each year during the first weekend of October.

Does 60 miles of riding sound good to you? If it does, the long route to Washburn and through Cornucopia will get you to the rugged heart of the peninsula. Note several fine overviews of the Apostle Islands along County K. The loop is the route of the Ambulance 60, a popular citizen's bicycle race, held in mid-August. If it seems like too much for one day, you'll find overnight camping in Cornucopia and at Big Rock Wayside Park near Washburn, which nestles in a beautiful river gorge. It can also be reached via mountain bike on Jammer Hill Road, which has a good dirt surface except for occasional sandy spots. At one point, you'll be treated to a panoramic view of Madeline Island and Mt. Ashwabay.

If you're riding with children, or if you're in the mood for a less demanding ride, buy a ferry boat ticket and enjoy the excursion to Madeline Island. As you roll your bike off the ferry, you'll see a stockaded log building with huge moose antlers on the gable. This is the State Historical Society's Madeline Island Museum. Open June 15 through September 15 daily, it preserves the area's long and fascinating history.

The island was once the center of the most powerful Indian nation in North America: the Ojibiwa. Through their alliance with the French, they controlled the fur trade, keeping the Sioux to the south and the Iroquois to the east from entering the region. The French establish-

ed a trading post at La Pointe in 1693, and each summer witnessed the departure of great 14-man canoes, laden with several tons of furs, to Montreal. The museum has an extensive collection of Indian and fur trade artifacts, as well as items from the logging and sailing era, including an incredible French brass and cut glass lighthouse lamp.

A short distance to the east near the modern marina you can visit the Indian Mission Cemetery. The mission church stood near this unique little graveyard in the 19th century. Some of the tiny, moss-covered spirit houses still stand above Indian graves. These small structures represent an accommodation between Christian and Ojibwa beliefs; the Indians believed that the spirit of the deceased lingered on earth for four days and needed food and shelter—a spirit house—during that time. The air is so pure here that the epitaphs on the marble stones of the French fur traders, scattered around the cemetery, are crisp and legible—"Seraphim LaComble, Died December 1840. This stone is erected by his friends as a measure of respect and esteem."

On a road bike you can still enjoy the scenery on an eight-mile paved loop. I strongly recommend taking the effort needed to get your skinny tires through the sandy roads that lead to Big Bay state and town parks. Both offer camping and access to the white, sandy crescent beach that stretches between them, yet their characters are quite different. From the town park you have an overview of a lagoon and tamarack bog—a haven for wildlife. The focus of the state park is the wave-battered red sandstone rock formations that jut out into Lake Superior.

There are several taverns and restaurants at La Pointe, but don't get caught inside when the sun is going down. A Lake Superior sunset is one of the most refreshing experiences you'll ever have.

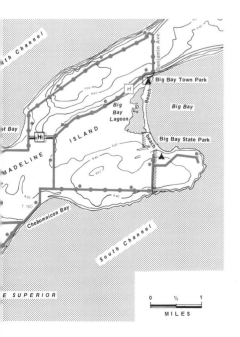

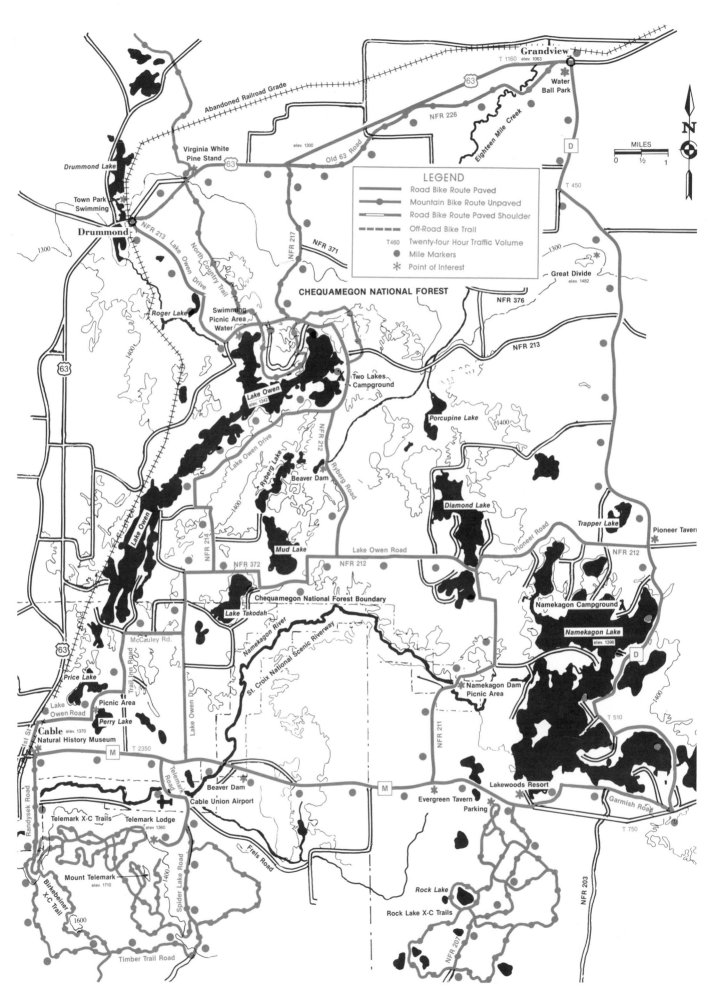

CHEQUAMEGON NATIONAL FOREST RIDE

Here is your chance to see how many ways you can mispronounce Chequamegon. When the French phoneticized the Ojibwa word for beaver, whose fur they sought, they pronounced it sha-WA-ma-gon. I fell under the spell of this fascinating collage of lakes, kettle bogs and undulating forest years ago, and I can guarantee that one visit will lead to another.

The longest on-road route shown here is 50 miles and corresponds to the route of the Grandview Firehouse Fifty Bicycle Road Race and Tour, a citizen's race (meaning an event for everyone, no racing license required) held during the first weekend of August by the Grandview Volunteer Fire Department. This festive race has become so popular they have had to limit entries to 500 riders. The shorter routes wind through rolling terrain where wind-shaped white pines are silhouetted against the sky and low spots are filled with sparkling lakes and bogs dotted with tamarack trees.

A visit to the Natural History Museum in Cable is a good way to identify animals you may encounter on your ride: the highly maneuverable broadwing hawk hunts from tree limb perches, and can surprise you by swooping aerobatically over the road; loons favor the abundance of quiet protected lakes, and as you pedal silently along, you may hear their mysterious calls filtering through the woods.

The Evergreen Tavern, visible from the intersection of County M and NFR 211, is the only facility beyond Cable, but well worth a stop. Food consists of popcorn and bar snacks that can be munched while watching song birds feeding outside the windows. You are welcome to join the Chequama Mamas Bicycle Club on their weekly Thursday ride. They resolve the "eat to ride" or "ride to eat" dilemma by taking the shortest, smoothest route to the home of whomever happens to be hosting the potluck dinner. Check with Gary or Sara at the Creative Touch Shop at Telemark Lodge about the point of departure for

the rides. They usually get underway about 6 p.m.

For any reason, a stop at Telemark, just east of Cable, is a must. Aside from being an architectural masterpiece, the 200-room resort is part of the vanguard of the citizen's athletic movement. In 1973 Telemark's creator, Tony Wise, played a hunch. Going against prevailing opinions that Americans were lazy and would not ski unless they could ride chair lifts, he opened cross-country ski trails and inaugurated the first American Birkebeiner citizen's cross-country marathon, to which 53 hardy skiers responded. Today, completing the "Birkie" is considered the mark of a skier. Now the greatest skiing celebration ever held in North America, it attracts thousands of participants and specatators.

Telemark's extensive system of cross-country ski trails is also great for fall mountain biking. During the spring and summer, trails often have standing water and are not mowed. A trail map and a compass are a must for following this complicated trail system. Signs are good, but the profusion of intersecting logging roads make it necessary to keep orienting yourself.

The Birkie trail is as challenging to the mountain biker as it is to the cross-country skier. It is also part of the course of the Chequamegon 40, a 40-mile mountain bike race from the Main Street of Hayward to Lakewoods Resort on Lake Namekagon. The event is part of the Chequamegon Fat Tire Festival held in late September. Near Lakewoods you can ride the National Forest's Rock Lake Ski Trails, winding through lake-dotted, rolling forest terrain. They are well marked with "you are here" maps, and maintained during the summer.

If these tastes of the Chequamegon are not enough, you can take on the North Country Trail. The narrow hiking trail is mountain biking at its toughest, and an average speed of four miles an hour is not bad. Proficiency with a compass is essential on this rough-surfaced, sparsely-marked trail, which passes the

An old railroad tressle overlooks the Chequamegon National Forest.

Twin Lakes Campground on Lake Owen and a magnificent stand of virgin white pines near Drummond. East of Lake Owen drive the trail runs through the Porcupine Lake Wilderness, where the use of any vehicles including mountain bikes is not allowed.

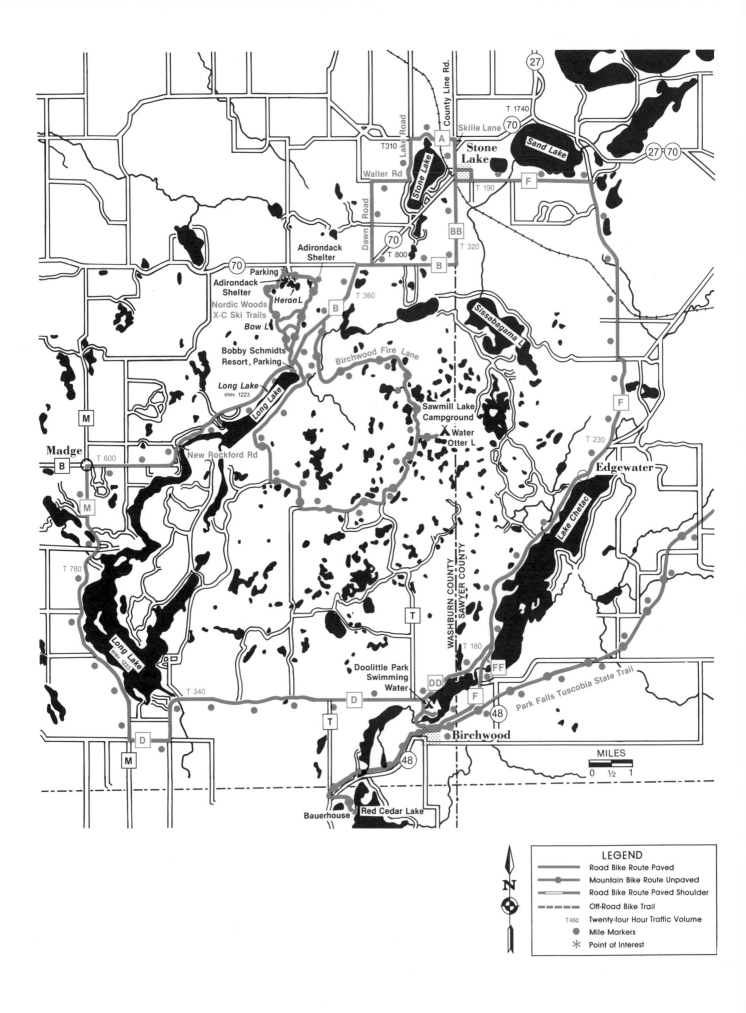

27

T 1740
Skille Lane
70

Sand Lake

27 70

A
Stone
Lake

Lake Road
County Line Rd.

T310
Walter Rd

T 190
F

Stone Lake

70

BB
T 320

B
T 800

Adirondack
Shelter

Dawn Road

70
Parking
Adirondack
Shelter
Nordic Woods
X-C Ski Trails
Heron L

Bow L

B
T 360

Birchwood Fire Lane

Sissabagama L

Bobby Schmidts
Resort, Parking

Long Lake
elev. 1223

Long Lake

F
T 230

Sawmill Lake
Campground
✕ Water
Otter L

Edgewater

M

Madge
B
T 600

New Rockford Rd

Lake Chetac

M

T 780

WASHBURN COUNTY
SAWYER COUNTY

T
T 180

Long Lake
elev. 1223

FF

Doolittle Park
Swimming
Water

DD
D

F
Park Falls Tuscobia State Trail

T 340

48

T

D

Birchwood

M

48

MILES
0   ½   1

Bauerhouse   Red Cedar Lake

LONG LAKE RIDE

A glance at the map will quickly tell you that Long Lake is not the only beautiful body of water along this route. The area owes its rolling hills and clear lakes with their elongated shapes to the meeting of two massive ice sheets during the last glacial epoch. Natural formations split the continental ice sheet into many sister lobes near its fringe. This division can be traced northward to the rugged Bayfield peninsula, which separated the ice into the Superior lobe to the west and the Chippewa lobe to the east. It was the parallel grinding of these rivers of ice that brought about the linear nature of the big lakes. Huge blocks of ice, buried in the rubble, pocked the landscape with hundreds of small lakes and bogs.

The payoff for the bicycle tourist is interesting—but not extreme—riding terrain that is a natural haven for wildlife. The land does not lend itself to farming due to its rugged character. The wildness has attracted enough people, however, to dot the area with a smattering of resorts and several towns that provide the bicyclist with essential services. Country stores at Madge and Edgewater augment the small communities of Stone Lake and Birchwood. The Just Rite Cafe in the latter town served me an outstanding order of French toast one morning; plan plenty of time to enjoy the food if you stop here.

You can camp and swim at Doolittle Park on the edge of Birchwood. This interesting little park is directly across the lake from a sawmill, and from here you can watch the operation of this typical Northwoods industry. If you keep your eyes open, you might spot a floating island drifting on one of the lakes. These phenomena are detached sections of bog—masses of sphagnum moss studded with tamarack trees—which can cause problems. A few years ago, on a lake south of here, one of these transient islands changed a resident's lakefront property into inland property overnight. It defied the tug of 17 motorboats, which tried to tow it away. Then one day it just up and floated off.

Those with ten-speeds will be able to put together long, scenic rides wtih stops at many lakes and several campgrounds. Mountain bike riders will find even more adventures in this area. The Park Falls Tuscobia State Trail can be picked up at Birchwood. This old railroad grade, originally envisioned as a bicycle/snowmobile trail, was only developed fully to serve snowmobilers. When the snow melts, mountain bikers can have the trail all to themselves. For the really ambitious, the next town to the east, Couderay, is only 20 miles away. You can combine a shorter route with outstanding dining by following the trail southwest out of town. The reconstruction at Highway 48 obliterated the railroad grade in places, making a more interesting ride as the trail rolls with the terrain.

Off on a side road four miles southwest of Birchwood you will find the Bauerhaus, a massive log and fieldstone example of "up north" opulence on the shore of Red Cedar Lake. Once the summer retreat of a Chicago millionaire, the Bauerhaus now serves food and drinks. The rambling log structure cascades down to the lake edge; you enter on the second level following a balcony, which overlooks the vaulted great hall with its massive two-story fireplace.

For another enjoyable tour, turn your fat tires to the Birchwood Fire Lane, which will lead you on a circular route to Sawmill Lake Campground, a gorgeous little spot where you can really get away from it all. If tougher terrain is your meat, try the Nordic Woods cross-country ski trail system. You can get on the trail across County B from Bobby Schmidt's Resort. The trail is rough but beautiful and you should plan on spending several hours if you want to cover the eight-and-a-half-mile loop. Plan on a little more time and you can rest at an adirondack shelter at the north end of Alpine Lake.

Birch trees and clear lakes line this beautiful Northwoods route.

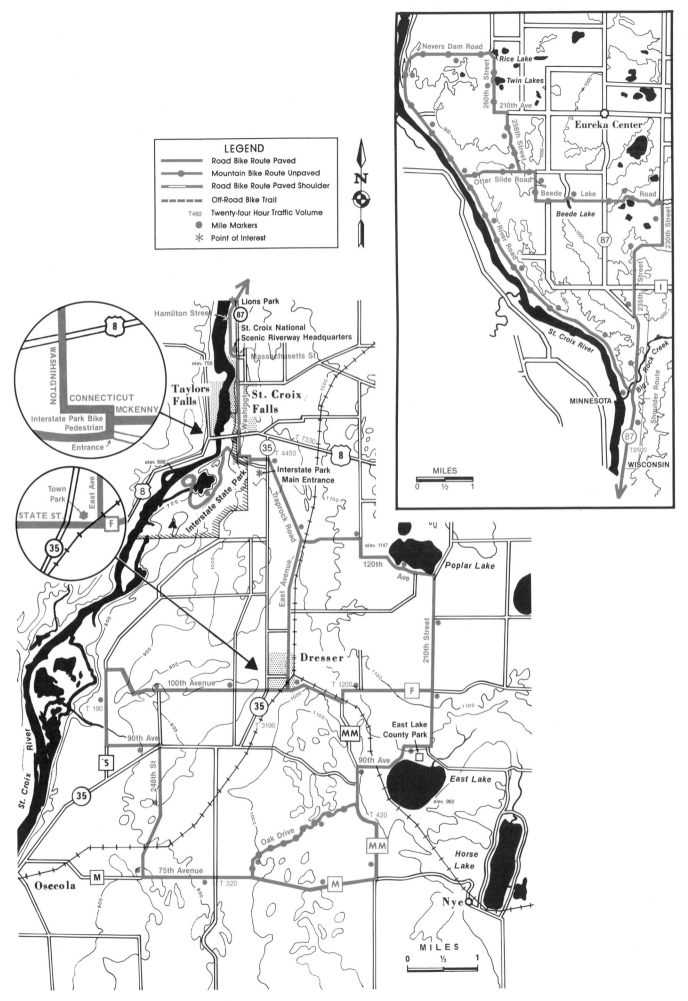

LEGEND

Road Bike Route Paved
Mountain Bike Route Unpaved
Road Bike Route Paved Shoulder
Off-Road Bike Trail
T460   Twenty-four Hour Traffic Volume
●   Mile Markers
✳   Point of Interest

N

Nevers Dam Road

Rice Lake

Twin Lakes

Eureka Center

260th Street

210th Ave

256th Street

Otter Slide Road

Beede   Lake   Road

Beede Lake

87

230th Street

235th Street

River Road

St. Croix River

Big Rock Creek

Shoulder Route

MINNESOTA

87

T2500

WISCONSIN

MILES

0   ½   1

8

WASHINGTON

CONNECTICUT

MCKENNY

Interstate Park Bike Pedestrian

Entrance

Hamilton Street

Lions Park

87

St. Croix National Scenic Riverway Headquarters

Massachusetts St

elev. 755

Taylors Falls

St. Croix Falls

Washington

elev. 688

8

Town Park

East Ave

STATE ST.

35

F

35

Interstate Park Main Entrance

35

T 4450

T 7330

8

700

Interstate State Park

elev. 1147

120th Ave

Poplar Lake

1100

Traprock Road

East Avenue

210th Street

1000

800

900

900

Dresser

100th Avenue

T 190

T 1200

F

35

90th Ave

T 3190

1100

1100

East Lake County Park

MM

90th Ave

East Lake

elev. 960

S

248th St

35

T 420

St. Croix River

1000

Oak Drive

MM

Horse Lake

75th Avenue

M

Osceola

T 320

M

Nye

MILES

0   ½   1

ST. CROIX RIDE

At Interstate Park, your first sight of the dramatic gorge of the St. Croix River is sure to leave you in awe—both of the power of nature's hand and of those who had the vision to preserve this place. It seems appropriate that Interstate was the first Wisconsin State Park created in 1900 as a joint venture with Minnesota, which manages the park's western shore. The beauty and significance of the St. Croix, confined within sheer, 200 foot walls of fractured lava rock, was further protected during the past decade when it was designated the first National Scenic Riverway.

As a place to ride a bicycle, the surrounding area is hard to beat for skinny and fat-tired bicyclists alike. If you are pedaling on balloon tires head north along River Road (see inset), which closely traces the course of the great water highway that is little changed since the days of the fur trade. Near Lions Park stands a historical marker commemorating the Battle of St. Croix Falls, which raged through the gorge for days. The clash took place in 1770, and was one of the epic battles between the Ojibwa nation, centered around Madeline Island in Lake Superior, and the combined forces of their traditional enemies, the Sioux and Fox. The tribes were fighting to see who would control the fur trade. The Ojibiwa succeeded by driving the Sioux out of Wisconsin and the Fox into the southern part of the state.

It is interesting to think about the fur trade's mixing of two vastly different cultures—the French and the Indians—as you bicycle along the river route. To the Indians, life's needs were finite and easily obtained. To the French and later the English, one could never be rich enough—the Indians remarked that France must be a horrible place if traders traveled such great distances and endured tremendous hardship just to obtain animal skins. Ultimately the French became more like the Indians rather than the other way around. The illiteracy of the Indians and the voyageurs leaves us mainly with the writings of the

The St. Croix River is confined within sheer, 200-foot walls of rock.

missionaries, the sons of Europe's upper crust who carried the cross into the wilderness at the fervor of the anti-reformation, as a study of these times. To most of the missionaries the Indian lifestyle was disgusting, and living among them was a trial to bear. To the voyageur, who was usually propelled into the New World from the lowest ranks of a medieval society, Indian life was a welcome change. The missionaries remarked that one of their main obstacles in the conversion of the savages was that the traders behaved just like them.

Riding inland from the river you will find the rolling, lake- and bog-pocked landscape that characterizes glacial moraine. You may enjoy visiting the Ice Age Interpretive Center, which is open daily at Interstate Park, to learn about the two glaciers that pushed into this area. The one from the west left gray-hued moraines and the other, coming down from the northeast, left red deposits. The magnitude of these ice sheets is difficult to comprehend: after 10,000 years the land is still rebounding from its weight at the rate of about an inch each century.

The river gorge is post-glacial, but its existence is a direct result of the glacier's demise. As the eastern ice sheet melted back into the basin of Lake Superior, the drain got plugged, and the meltwater in the west end of the lake rose to 700 feet above its present level. When it finally broke through to the south the torrent cut through seven layers of lava like a chainsaw through a stack of magazines. One of Interstate Park's most fascinating remnants of this hydraulic extravaganza are the potholes bored into the rock by swirling boulders, which had become captured by whirlpools. These impressive signatures of the event are as deep as eighty feet and can be found up to a hundred feet above the present river level.

The town of St. Croix Falls makes a pleasant stop on your ride. Being faced with the decision of choosing between Jahn's Restaurant and the Friendly Valley Bakery across the street, I did the only logical thing: I stopped in the bakery for pastry and coffee before my ride and enjoyed the homemade soup at Jahn's when I got back.

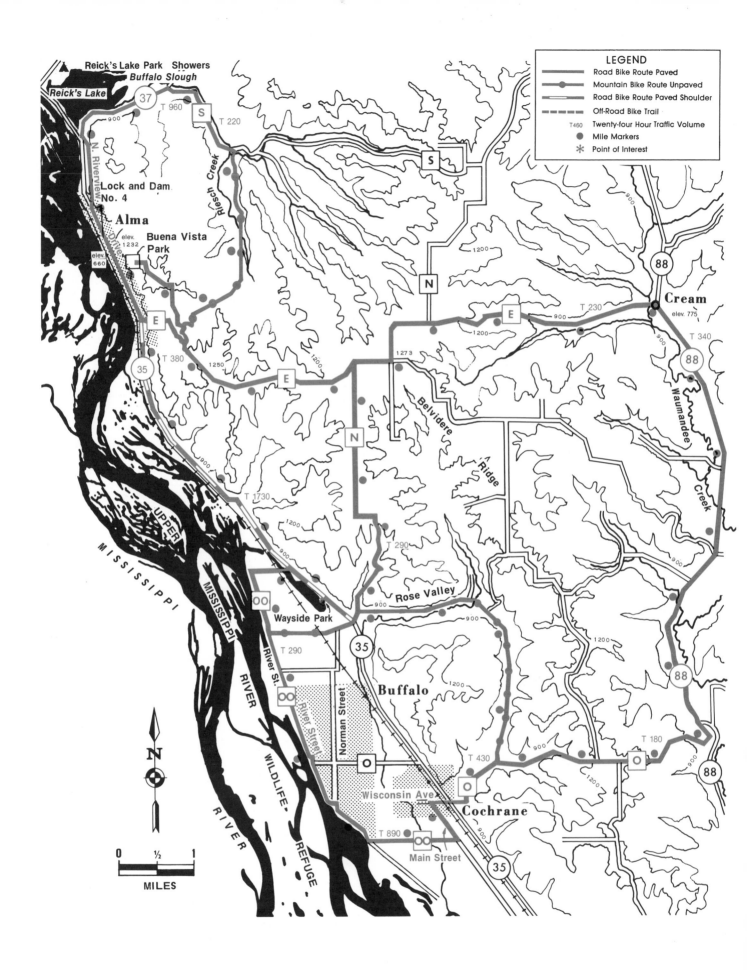

LEGEND
Road Bike Route Paved
Mountain Bike Route Unpaved
Road Bike Route Paved Shoulder
Off-Road Bike Trail
T460 Twenty-four Hour Traffic Volume
Mile Markers
* Point of Interest

Reick's Lake Park Showers
Buffalo Slough
Reick's Lake
37
T 960
T 220
S
N. Riverview
Lock and Dam No. 4
Alma
elev. 1232
Buena Vista Park
elev. 660
35
T 380
1250
1200
E
E
S
N
900
1200
E
T 230
Cream
elev. 775
88
T 340
88
1273
Belvidere Ridge
Waumandee Creek
N
T 1730
1200
900
T 290
Rose Valley
900
Wayside Park
900
T 290
River St.
River Street
35
Buffalo
1200
1200
Norman Street
900
T 180
88
O
T 430
O
O
88
Wisconsin Ave.
Cochrane
T 890
Main Street
35

UPPER
MISSISSIPPI
MISSISSIPPI
RIVER
WILDLIFE REFUGE
RIVER

N

0   ½   1
MILES

BELVIDERE RIDGE RIDE

Picture-perfect describes the scenery along the ridgetops and through the tranquil valleys of this ride. In the river town of Alma, there is an increased pride and awareness of the area's heritage, particularly in the Greek Revival, Federal and Victorian style homes and buildings nestled against the warm beige Mississippi River bluffs.

Ridges can either be climbed or cleverly avoided on this tour. If you take on the challenge of the awe-inspiring bluffs, you will eventually find yourself 600 feet above the level of the Mississippi. In case the condition of your legs makes brain rather than brawn the key to an enjoyable trip, you can outsmart the terrain by taking an out-and-back ramble on the newly paved shoulder along Highway 35. If you're riding on fat tires, take advantage of the grand scenery by cruising the gravel road through Rose Valley, where two valleys have united—an unusual geological phenomenon.

On the level ground of the river terrace, you'll be treated to an intimate view of the Mississippi. The bottomland here is a National Wildlife Refuge, and its backwater sloughs are choked with lush green water plants. It's easy to spot the occasional sentinel-like great blue heron watching over the floating mass. The silence is frequently interrupted by the highballing freight trains of the Burlington Northern. The deafening rumble of the air horns against the river bluff will convince you that profitable railroad lines in America are not dead.

Buena Vista Park is a great place to begin a more ambitious tour and a point of interest visitors shouldn't miss, even if it means crawling up the bluff. Sit and relax here at the end of a ride. Your reward is a view of the Mississippi that will leave you with an indelible impression of this avenue of commerce. From the considerable height of the park, you can watch as North America's greatest river hauls the tremendous bounty of the plains. In seeming miniature, tugboats maneuver groups of barges, some as long as several football fields, through a maize of green islands and the locks of dam No. 4 just below. You can see what is going on in just about every backyard in Alma as well. Bring liquid refreshment along as there is no water available at the park.

Compared to the climb up the bluff, the roll along the ridgetop will seem flat. If you head east from Alma you will be treated to a two-mile downhill run into the intimate, narrow valley that leads to the unincorporated town of Cream. On this visit, I finally took time to stop and check out the Ponderosa Tavern, Cream's only business establishment, and one filled with soft strains of old country and western tunes from a juke box. Riding south of Cream, you'll enjoy close contact with the beauty of the valley floor, typical of so many sections of this tour. As you climb out of the valley heading west on County O, there's a grand overview of the hills that cradle Waumandee Creek.

For those hankering for real mountain bike adventure, the old one-lane dirt road winding down from Buena Vista Park along Riesch Creek is made to order. After following a farm field for a short distance, the path plunges into the woods in a steep, twisting descent punctuated by washouts and abandoned farmsteads. Paralleling the dry stream bed, the road eventually junctions with County S after passing a strange-looking ginseng farm, with its lath canopies over the raised plant beds.

County S leads you down to Highway 37, where the route traces the edge of an incredible expanse of lily pads called Buffalo Slough. On the northwest shore of the slough is Reick's Lake Park, a great little camping spot featuring the luxury of showers. Just before the junction with Highway 35, you can avoid the traffic by turning south onto the old road now named North Riverview Drive. This exits onto Alma's main street near the Burlington Inn, an old railroad hotel that, in its present incarnation, is an excellent little restaurant.

If you like 19th century luxury more than

Egrets and many other kinds of waterfowl can be seen along the Mississippi River and its sloughs.

camping, you can find accommodations at the Laue House, a restored Victorian mansion near the south end of town. For breakfast, you might consider hopping on a boat. A small ferry service, which operates near Dam No. 4 to haul fishermen, will carry you to a restaurant on the far shore for your morning meal.

GOOSE ISLAND RIDE

If you like grand scenery and sleepy little towns, this ride is for you. The laid-back character of the area belies the fact that it's just a few miles from the busy city of La Crosse.

Those who choose to start a trip in this urban environment can reasonably do so now. A paved shoulder has been added to Highway 35 from the city to Goose Island. This beautiful county park is one of the most picturesque spots on the Mississippi River. Its lattice of backwater sloughs is the home of egrets and herons who dwell among the lush, yellow-flowered water plants. You can rent a canoe for a closer look or enjoy the view from a campsite or picnic area through a pair of binoculars. The backdrop for this lovely spot is the towering wooded bluffs of the Mississippi River Valley, and it is on these ridges and side valleys that real bicycle adventure begins. You will feel like the king of the mountain as you survey La Crosse, sprawled across the river terrace below, from the height of Grandad Bluff Park.

Not everyone has the enthusiasm or ability to challenge the 300-foot plus climbs out of the valley. For those of you in this category, there is a nearly flat loop running east out of Stoddard on Highway 162 and Cedar Valley Road that will treat you to some of the best valley and Mississippi scenery without the toll of leg-straining uphill climbs. On my visit in mid-July, I found these lightly traveled roads lined with bright orange day lillies and a myriad of other wildflowers.

Bicyclists who are strong of limb and willpower can tackle as many hills and miles as desired by ranging eastward on one or more of the tour's loops. The reward will be a trip through winding valley scenery that unravels before you with steep, forested side walls occasionally broken with bright sandstone outcroppings. The high percentage of maple trees make the tour even more extraordinary during the fall. If you travel far enough you will wind up in the ridgetop community of Newberg Corners. The town's only enterprises, a tavern and a country store, will seem like real oasis between open, shelterless farmland.

For a more sophisticated taste of rural culture, visit the town of Coon Valley. Each year in mid-August, the Soil Conservation Festival commemorates the historic efforts of the community to conserve their fertile soil.

Coon Valley has lots to offer the bicyclist. You can camp or picnic on the banks of Coon Creek at Veteran's Park and buy your provisions at Anderson's Dry Goods Store, a real old-fashioned general store where they still stack cans in pyramid displays. A rail-mounted stepladder slides along the wall for hard-to-reach items. At the Windmill Inn Restaurant and Museum, located in a fine old red-brick building on Main Street, you can enjoy a snack and inspect a turn-of-the-century bicycle that has rods rather than a chain driving the rear wheel.

For you mountain bike riders who find that roads like the one up Mowhawk Valley aren't tough enough, you can tackle rugged off-road riding on the cross-country ski trails at Bluebird Recreation Area. A $1 area use fee allows you to ride the trails, quench your thirst at a well-stocked snack bar and cool off in the swimming pool, which all riders can enjoy at this pleasant, privately-operated campground.

Ridges, bluffs, and valleys border the Mississippi, forming a backdrop for bicycling adventure.

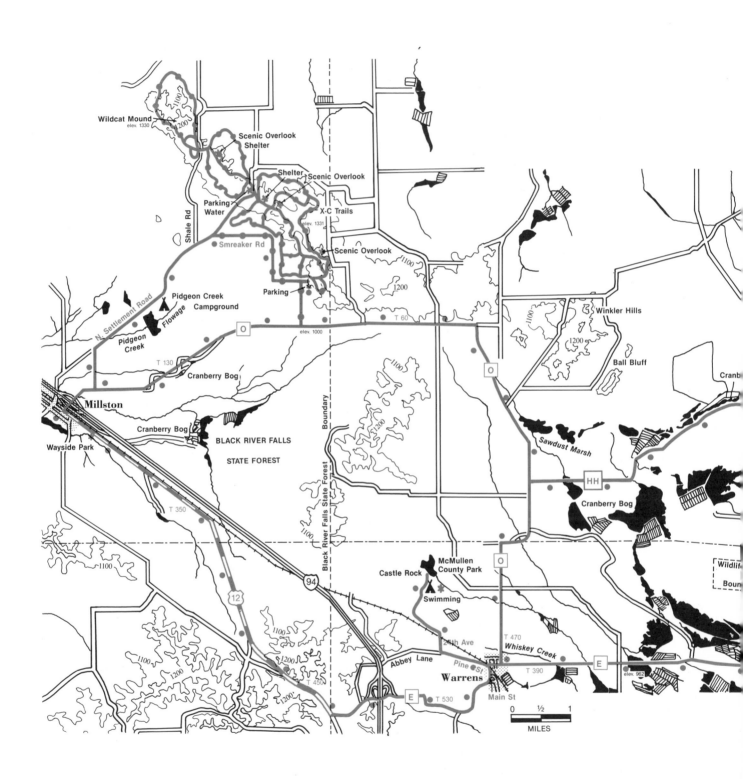

Wildcat Mound
elev. 1330

Scenic Overlook
Shelter

Shelter
Scenic Overlook

Parking
Water

X-C Trails
elev. 1331

Shale Rd

Smreaker Rd

Scenic Overlook

Parking

elev. 1000

Pidgeon Creek
Campground

N. Settlement Road

Pidgeon
Creek Flowage

T 130

Cranberry Bog

O

T 60

1100

1200

1100

Winkler Hills

Ball Bluff

Cranb

O

1200

Millston

Cranberry Bog

Wayside Park

BLACK RIVER FALLS
STATE FOREST

Boundary

Black River Falls State Forest

T 350

1100

1200

1100

Sawdust Marsh

HH

Cranberry Bog

Wildlife
Boun

1100

94

12

McMullen
County Park

Castle Rock

Swimming

O

1100

1200

T 470

Whiskey Creek

24th Ave

Abbey Lane

Pine St

Warrens

E

T 530

Main St

T 390

E

elev. 962

1100

1200

1200

T 450

0   ½   1
MILES

BLACK RIVER FALLS STATE FOREST RIDE

For those of you who are unaware of the importance of the bright, tart berry usually associated with pilgrims, turkey and holiday feasting, this ride—a loop through the cranberry bog country straddling the Jackson and Monroe County line—will be an education. The cranberry is the only berry native exclusively to North America. Around Warrens, its cultivation is the only type of agriculture possible. It grows naturally in the cold water bogs the glacier left behind; Massachusetts and Wisconsin are the nation's leading producers.

Riding east from Warrens, you'll pedal through miles of commercial and wild bogs in lowlands cradled by rugged hills, which were once islands rising out of a great glacial lake. The character of the bogs changes with the seasons from an emerald green in summer to a rusty brown in the fall. The wild bogs are also the home of tiny orchids and the insect-eating pitcher plant. Fall is harvest time for the commercial operations, and after the berries are raked loose, the rice-paddy-like bogs are flooded. The floating fruit is then swept onto conveyor belts.

Warrens celebrates the harvest with the annual Cranberry Festival in late September or early October. An estimated 30,000 visitors overwhelm the tiny, one-tavern, one-grocery community to sample cranberry breads, cookies, pies, cakes, juices, carameled cranberries, and even distinctly-flavored honey from bog bees. Commercial cranberry operations lead tours. Even on less-crowded weekends, you can find some of the cranberry delights, and you'll stand a better chance of getting a bowl of the good homemade soup served at the Village Inn. Either way, stock up before leaving town as you won't find so much as a tavern on the eastern loop of this route.

McMullen Park, just north of Warrens, is a beautiful spot offering camping, picnicking and swimming in a small lake surrounded by an oak and pine forest. Camping is available in the very tourable Black River Falls State Forest. Be sure to visit Grandma Smreker's Truck Stop in Milliston. Before the interstate was built, Highway 12 was the main road between Minneapolis and Chicago. Grandma's, a relic from that period, still hangs on, probably because of its cozy restaurant or the fact that they still sell candy and peanuts by the pound. Their motel is also a period piece with rates to match.

The cross-country trail system north of Milliston offers the mountain bike rider 14 miles of wide-mowed trails and the opportunity to scale some of the ridges that silhouette the horizon. From the ridge overlooks, it's easy to imagine the time when the hills in the vast flat sea of forest stretching out below were islands. The well-designed downhill runs can be taken at speeds that make your arms tingle from the vibrating handlebars. The trails are well-marked, but bring a compass anyway. When I rode the trails I found my self circling the same loop twice before going out to the road in order to get back. In the winter on skis, I had no trouble at all locating the exit.

Cranberry Bog

HH

JACKSON COUNTY
MONROE COUNTY

MEADOW VALLEY WILDLIFE AREA

T 90

E

T 100

173

N

LEGEND

———	Road Bike Route Paved
——•——	Mountain Bike Route Unpaved
▭▭▭	Road Bike Route Paved Shoulder
- - - -	Off-Road Bike Trail
T460	Twenty-four Hour Traffic Volume
●	Mile Markers
✳	Point of Interest

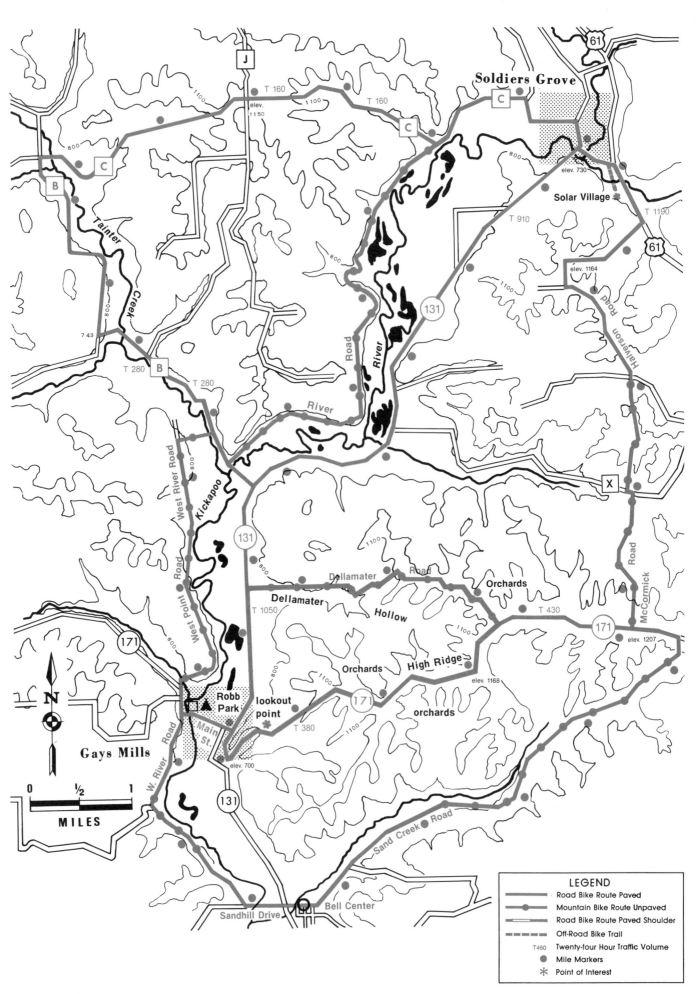

LEGEND

	Road Bike Route Paved
	Mountain Bike Route Unpaved
	Road Bike Route Paved Shoulder
	Off-Road Bike Trail
T460	Twenty-four Hour Traffic Volume
●	Mile Markers
✳	Point of Interest

KICKAPOO VALLEY RIDE

Here's an opportunity to explore a land of contrasts. The valley of the Kickapoo presents the bicyclist with more than ridgetop and river bottom scenery; there is also the contrast between a rural small town rooted in the last century and a futuristic town that foretells the next century.

Ever since the first Dogpatcher took a swig of Kickapoo Joy Juice in the comic strip, "Li'l Abner," the Kickapoo has been synonymous with a kind of rustic lifestyle. In fact, not a great deal of what is usually referred to as progress has ever hit the valley. With any sudden runoff from the steep valley sides, the normally lazy meanders of the Kickapoo River overflow their banks. Not the sort of thing to attract new residents or businesses.

In Soldiers Grove, however, things have changed. As I pedaled down the old Main Street, I passed vacant stores and buildings, one-time flood victims. But turning south onto Highway 61, I found myself in "America's First Solar Village." All of the buildings, rising out of the flood plain, harness the sun's energy: the post office, gas station, supermarket, bank, library and the Country Garden Restaurant. I took temporary refuge from the midday July sun in the latter. The food is typically American fare, but quite good.

In the adjoining tap room, I found an old Norwegian couple reminiscing about the bygone custom of *julebucking*. This Norwegian trick-or-treat was perpetrated between Christmas and New Years. Costumed folks would visit neighbors who served them drinks and tried to guess their identity. The tradition has languished, but deserves to be revived.

An etched mirror, depicting the store fronts on old Main Street, lines the tap room, and after awhile I worked the conversation around to the new town versus the old. The only complaint was that a few merchants had taken the federal relocation money and started businesses in other towns rather than reinvesting in Soldiers Grove.

One of many quaint villages nestled among ridges and hollows in the Kickapoo Valley.

You're not likely to find much else that is new on your tour of the Kickapoo Valley. There is certainly no new pavement. While this won't bother those of you with mountain bikes, narrow-tired riders will be happier on County B and C and State Highways 171 and 131, with the caution that the latter, while not heavily traveled, does get busy on weekends. Fat-tired riders will have the run of River Road, also known as the Kickapoo Cow Path. This pioneer road has changed little since covered-wagon days, and its serpentine route will offer you the best view of the equally snaky Kickapoo.

The real test of your mountain- or road-biking ability will come when you climb out of the valley. Conquering a hill under your own steam is usually a reward in itself. On the ridges east of Gays Mills, you will have the additional treat of a pleasant roll through miles of apple orchards. If you are there during the third week in May, the trees will be covered with fragrant, snowy-white blossoms. On the first weekend of October, the Gays Mills Apple Festival marks the harvest. The bright red fruit is turned into pies, turnovers or sold *au natural*. The event attracts droves of visitors, so bicyclists that weekend will feel most comfortable riding the back roads.

Bridgeport

Wisconsin *River*

LEGEND
Road Bike Route Paved
Mountain Bike Route Unpaved
Road Bike Route Paved Shoulder
Off-Road Bike Trail
T460 Twenty-four Hour Traffic Volume
Mile Markers
* Point of Interest

800

1000

35

Lookout Point
elev. 1149

C

Wyalusing State Park

C

C

18

CX

GRANT COUNTY

T 440

T 510

X

X

X

P

Patch Grove

Wyalusing

Glass Hollow

35

133

X

P

Sandy Creek

1000

Bloomington

T 460

Bagley

A

T 690

1000

elev. 611

A

T 380

elev. 1060

133

T 220

Mississippi River

Dug Way Road

VV

U

35

1000

Rock School Rd

V

V

Glenhaven

Squirrel Hollow Rd.

Badger Rd

T 390

North Andover

T 370

V

1000

Duncan Road

Town Park

Mucallounge Road

Boot Hill

81

Good-Nuf Hollow Road

Kuenster Cr.

Beetown
elev. 800

800

fords

Ramsey Road

133

Garden Prairie Road

Atkinson Road

T 60

U

Rattle Snake Road

Lock and Dam No. 10

T 170

glen

VV

81

Rattlesnake Creek

800

Closing Dam Road

Nelson Dewey State Park

T 480

1000

0   1   2   3

I O W A

Lookout Points→

133

133

T 760

M I L E S

Stonefield Village

VV

N

swimming pool
Ferry to Iowa Shore

Cassville

800

133

COULEE COUNTRY RIDE

Playing pool is still free in Cassville's taverns. I'm not much of a pool player and neither were those I watched, but I found the incongruity of a German ethnic population living in a sleepy Mississippi River town and playing pool together somehow reassuring.

The weather can be hot on the river bottom. Camping on the blufftops at Wyalusing or Nelson Dewey state parks has been the only nonliquid prescription I could find to relieve the swelter. And the profusion of Indian mounds told me I was not the first to find this cool resting spot.

The axiom about no free lunch is easily applied to bicycling in this part of the state. There's a lot of up. If you have adventure in your soul, however, you're sure to enjoy the thrill of hurtling down miles of shaded coulee roads—the speed and swatches of sunlight flickering through the trees make you think you're watching an old-time movie. It's worth grinding up hills for.

Mountain bikes, with their special low gears, are made for this country, and a variety of rides can be put together on easy-going, gravel-surfaced roads. An out-and-back cruise on Dug Way Road

will eliminate any long climbs. From it you can survey the lush backwater of the Mississippi and enjoy the quiet presence of great blue herons. As it snakes along the river bluff, this road also gives you a chance to ride underground, as at one point, it passes under a massive overhang. Dug Way is your ticket to Glenhaven. When I rolled into town, the volunteer fire department was in the midst of a "fund raiser" on the main street. A resilient bunch, they demonstrated that one way to fight solar fire is not with fire, but with cold beer. Rock School and Squirrel Hollow roads are tough ways to get out of town, but the latter takes you past a tiny park where a spring of pure water gushes out of the rock. Camping is allowed.

Another great ride for fat-tire fanciers follows the railroad grade north from Cassville along Closing Dam Road. If you keep your eyes open you will find a gorgeous little glen just off the road to the right. In serene shade, a tiny waterfall spills over the layered rock strata. Turning up narrow Good-Nuff Hollow Road, you will get to wash the dust off your tires by fording several small creeks crossing

the road. Between the fords is the ruin of a burned-out stone cottage whose exposed walls reveal the mason's skill.

Heading west, you can enjoy the scenery—rolling, ridgetop farmland and lovely valleys—on roads that lead to sleepy little Beetown. The town was named by a miner named Cyrus Alexander, who passed through the valley just after a tornado and found a 425-pound nugget of pure lead among the roots of an overturned bee tree.

Boot Hill Cemetery in Beetown still watches over the main street's taverns and grocery store. There is superb riding in outlying hills and valleys, if you have the gears. One of the finest loops follows County X and P down Glass Hollow to the river bottom, turning north through the town of Wyalusing and climbing three miles back up to the ridgetop where the state park is located. From Wyalusing lookout points, you can drink in the vast panorama of the confluence of the Wisconsin and Mississippi rivers, a view first described by Father Marquette over 300 years ago.

For a journey of a different type, you can travel back into the last century at Stonefield Village, a reconstruction operated by the State Historical Society of Wisconsin. From June through Labor Day, you can take a horse-drawn trip past living practitioners of bygone skills and crafts. The last two weekends of August the town commemorates harvest time with a steam-powered thresheree.

If you find the grandeur of the Mississippi compelling, you can hop the car ferry for a ride to the Iowa shore. Whether your interest runs toward history, scenery, wildlife, small town charm or just getting your heart rate up with some good, hard bicycling, you will find what you're looking for in Coulee Country.

Amish farmers in horse drawn wagons and buggies can often be seen throughout this lush countryside.

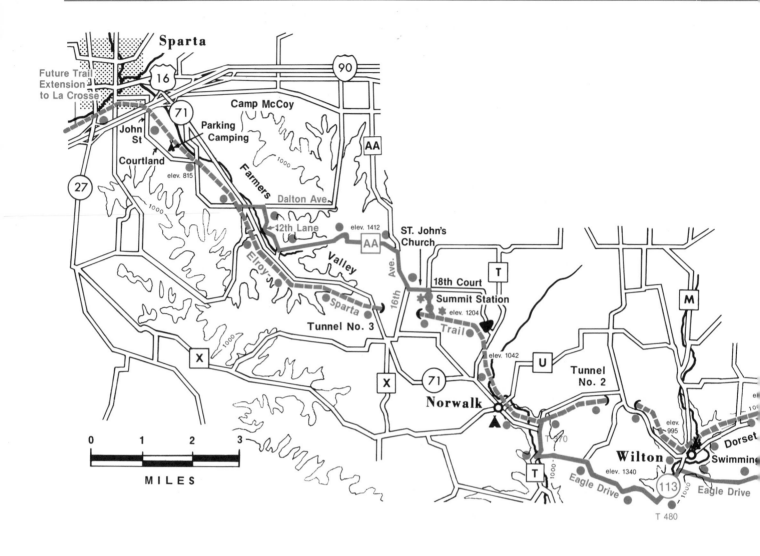

ELROY-SPARTA STATE TRAIL RIDE

When my children and I visited the Elroy-Sparta Trail in 1973, it was in its infancy. Our ride took us along the route of the abandoned Chicago and Northwestern Railroad the state had refurbished for bicycling and hiking. During our trip, we met a spry, retired postal worker named Boyd Wallace, cruising along on a balloon-tired relic. Boyd, a life-long Norwalk resident nicknamed "Trail Boss," knew everything about the railroad and the area's history. Listening to his stories—tales of floods, train wrecks and a different way of life—made the past come alive for us.

Today, the trail is a major success story. It attracts over 60,000 visitors annually and is a major economic factor and source of pride for the residents of the quiet towns through which it passes. On my recent visit I thought I would put a few miles on my mountain bike before stopping in Norwalk to see if I could locate Boyd Wallace. I should have known that the Trail Boss would be on the trail. Approaching tunnel No. 3, I found him helping bicyclists with the water pump and yarning about a little town named Summit Station that once stood on that very spot.

Boyd, still wearing his railroad cap and cut-off blue jeans, had not changed a bit. Except for one thing—Boyd had a skinny-tired ten speed. He told me he had gotten it shortly after we last met, and his speedometer showed 10,000 miles. It was a complete reversal. He was on skinny tires and I was rolling on the fat ones. But it was clear the ten intervening years in the saddle had done neither of us harm.

The three, 110-year-old tunnels are a big part of the appeal of the Elroy-Sparta. Tunnels No. 1 and 2 are about one-third mile long while No. 3 is over three-fourths

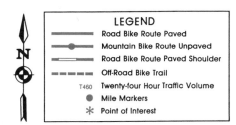

LEGEND
- ———— Road Bike Route Paved
- —•—•— Mountain Bike Route Unpaved
- ———— Road Bike Route Paved Shoulder
- ----- Off-Road Bike Trail
- T460 Twenty-four Hour Traffic Volume
- ● Mile Markers
- ✳ Point of Interest

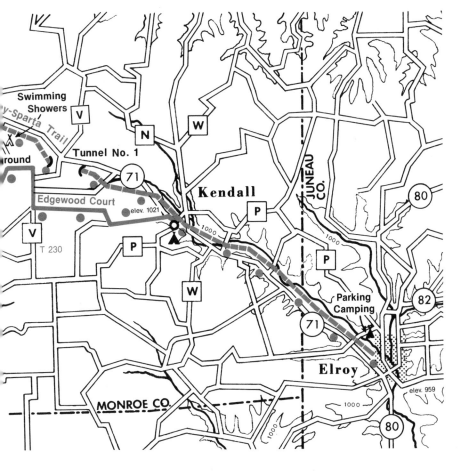

of a mile long. In each case, the cool, dark, damp passages are the setting for a walking-your-bike adventure of a unique kind. Wear a jacket even in summer and carry a flashlight for courage as much as for guidance. On a hot summer day, cool tunnel air makes a thick fog at the entrances heavy enough to block out light. In the middle of Tunnel 3, you will not be able to see either end.

Another factor in the success of the trail is the enthusiasm of the townsfolk. In the Wilton park on Sunday mornings from 7 to 10 a.m., the local Lion's Club whips up (for a modest price) a delicious all-you-can-eat pancake and sausage breakfast. If you can imagine a community that seems to revolve around serving the needs of bicyclists, this is it. Some businesses have been created because

of them. The Tunnel Trail Campground between Wilton and Kendall is a good example. This privately run campground (yes, they do have showers) serves the ever-increasing throng of bikers. Camping is also available at public sites at the ends of the trail and at town parks in Norwalk, Wilton and Kendall. The Sparta Chamber of Commerce is discussing plans for a bicycling hall of fame and looking forward to the future extension of the trail through the town and westward to the outskirts of La Crosse.

The fine crushed limestone of the trail is good for any type of bike tire. Mountain bikers will be able to take a few extra excursions to test their ultra low gears. Take the old Summit Road by crossing a small wooden bridge adjacent to the trail just across from the water pumps near the east end of Tunnel No. 3. The old gravel road leads through an emerald green valley, up a steep pitch and out onto the paved road at picturesque St. John's Church. It's a different world on the ridgetop. The farms stretch across the rolling tableland in orderly fashion, a contrast to the irregular fields tucked into the crannies of the intimate valleys below. East of Norwalk, Eagle Drive also offers ambitious bicyclists the kind of grueling climbs you can boast about and views of valleys you'll never forget.

ACKNOWLEDGEMENT

Thanks to the many friends and fellow bicyclists who, though too numerous to mention, have contributed so much to this product.

DEDICATION

To Dudley, who showed me how.

ILLUSTRATION CREDITS

FRONT COVER: Becky Mead / Inside Front Cover, Ginny Peifer / pg. 2, upper, Vern Arendt / pg. 2, right, Hans Pigorsch / pg. 2, bottom, Brent Nicastro / pg. 5-6, Phil Van Valkenberg / pg. 7, top, Ron Thompson / pg. 7, bottom, Phil Van Valkenberg / pg. 8, Phil Van Valkenberg / pg. 9, Vern Arendt / pg. 11, Phil Van Valkenberg / pg. 12-14, Ginny Peifer / pg. 16, top, Brent Nicastro / pg. 16, bottom, Steve Raymer / pg. 17, Phil Van Valkenberg / pg. 21, State Historical Society of Wisconsin / pg. 25, Brent Nicastro / pg. 27, Tom Riles / pg. 29, Wollersheim Winery / pg. 31, Jim Umhoefer / pg. 33, Wis. Division of Tourism / pg. 35, State Historical Society of Wisconsin / pg. 37, Robert Boyd / pg. 39, Edgar Mueller / pg. 41, Vern Arendt / pg. 43, Nancy Mead / pg. 45, Hans Pigorsch / pg. 49, Phil Van Valkenberg / pg. 51, Gary Garnet / pg. 53, Phil Van Valkenberg / pg. 55, Brent Nicastro / pg. 57, Jim Umhoefer / pg. 61, Phil Van Valkenberg / pg. 65, Ron Engh / pg. 67, Nancy Mead / pg. 71, Phil Van Valkenberg / pg. 73, upper, Nancy Mead / pg. 75, Brent Nicastro.

TRIP NOTES